A PLANTSMAN'S GUIDE TO

DELPHINIUMS

LESLIE COOPER

A
PLANTSMAN'S GUIDE TO
DELPHINIUMS
LESLIE COOPER

SERIES EDITOR
ALAN TOOGOOD

WARD LOCK

First published in Great Britain in 1990 by Ward
Lock Limited, Artillery House, Artillery Row,
London SW1P 1RT, a Cassell Company

House editor Denis Ingram

Text filmset in Times Roman
by Dorchester Typesetting
Printed and bound in Portugal by
Resopal

British Library Cataloguing in Publication Data

Cooper, Leslie
   A plantsman's guide to delphiniums.
   1. Gardens. Delphiniums
   I. Title
   635.9'33111

ISBN 0 7063 6833 9

Cover photograph: Delphinium 'Lock Leven'
Courtesy Nigel Moody.

CONTENTS

PUBLISHER'S NOTE

Readers are requested to note that in order to make the
text intelligible in both hemispheres, plant flowering
times, etc. are described in terms of seasons, not
months. The following table provides an approximate
'translation' of seasons into months for the two
hemispheres.

Northern Hemisphere		Southern Hemisphere
Mid-winter	= January	= Mid-summer
Late winter	= February	= Late summer
Early spring	= March	= Early autumn
Mid-spring	= April	= Mid-autumn
Late spring	= May	= Late autumn
Early summer	= June	= Early winter
Mid-summer	= July	= Mid-winter
Late summer	= August	= Late winter
Early autumn	= September	= Early spring
Mid-autumn	= October	= Mid-spring
Late autumn	= November	= Late spring
Early winter	= December	= Early summer

Captions for colour photographs on chapter-opening pages:

pp. 8-9 The delphiniums catch the eye, but notice the variety
of foliage in this mixed border.

pp. 22-23 Delphiniums and kniphofia in a beautiful corner at
'The Miller's House', owned by Mr and Mrs C. Pretzlik.

pp. 40-41 A stone's throw from Canterbury Cathedral, this
small garden illustrates how spectacular delphiniums can be.

pp. 64-65 All shades of delphiniums make Richard
Wainright's garden at 'The Heath' a joy to see.

pp. 74-75 Delphiniums in their majesty with the pink
Geranium endressi 'Wargrave pink' and yellow helianthus.

pp. 104-105 With a little planning other plants will come into
flower as the delphinium season comes to an end.

pp. 120-121 The yellow hemerocallis (daylilies) are an
excellent foreground foil for blue delphiniums.

Kennedys Garden Centres

ALPINES

FREE LEAFLET

A RAISED ALPINE BED

Many Alpine and Rock Garden Plants require so little space, that a large number of varieties can be grown in a very small space.

These plants mostly need an open sunny position which is well drained. Some plants (listed below) are shade tolerant, but it is best to avoid very shady areas as even these plants will not thrive.

Growing plants in a raised bed or trough will add an easily maintained feature to your patio or garden. Even the smallest garden has space for a miniature feature such as these. For plant selection see below.

Slow growing Shrubs and Conifers will add year round interest and colour to any Rock Garden. Pruning, where necessary should be carried out when the plant has flowered. Very little pruning should be necessary.

1. ALPINES FOR SPECIAL PLACES

a) **Plants for Sunny Places**
   Acaena in variety
   Alyssum in variety
   Arabis in variety
   Aubretia in variety
   Cerastium
   Crepis incana
   Dianthus in variety
   Erinus in variety
   Gypsophila in variety
   Helianthemum in variety
   Hypericum in variety
   Iberis in variety
   Linum in variety
   Pentstemon in variety
   Polygonum vaccinifolium
   Sedum in variety
   Sempervivum in variety
   Thymus in variety
   Veronica most varieties

b) **Shade tolerant plants**
   Acaena 'Blue Haze'
   Acaena buchananii
   Ajuga in variety
   Campanula in variety
   Cotula squalida
   Dodecatheon
   Gentiana septemfida
   Gypsophila in variety
   Iberis 'Snowflake'
   Lithosperum 'Heavenly Blue'
   Nierembergia rivularis
   Phlox-alpine types in variety
   Polygonum vaccinifolium
   Primula some varieties
   Thymus in variety
   Viola in variety

c) **Plants for growing between Paving Stones**
   Acaena buchananii
   Arenaria balearica
   Arenaria caespitosa 'Aurea'
   Cotula squalida
   Nierembergia rivularis
   Raoulia australis
   Sedum album 'Coral Carpet'
   Thymus all prostrate forms

d) **Trailing Plants**
   Alyssum in variety
   Arabis in variety

Arenaria montana
Aubretia in variety
Campanula 'Birch Hybrid'
Campanula 'G. F. Wilson'
Campanula portenschlagiana
Dianthus in variety
Dryas octopetela
Geranium 'Ballerina'
Geranium subcaulescens 'Splendens'
Gypsophila in variety
Helianthemum in variety
Hypericum polyphyllum Grandiflorum
Iberis 'Snowflake'
Lithosperum 'Heavenly Blue'
Pentstemon in variety
Phlox alpine varietic
Polygonum vaccinifolium
Saponaria ocymoides
Thymus in variety
Veronica in variety

e) **Ground Cover Plants**
   Acaena 'Blue Haze'
   Achilles tomentosa
   Ajuga in variety
   Arabis caucasica varieties
   Armeria maritime in variety
   Campanula 'Birch Hybrid'
   Campanula portenschlagiana
   Geranium subcaulescens 'Splendens'
   Gypsophila in variety
   Helianthemum in variety
   Iberis commutatum
   Lithospermum 'Heavenly Blue'
   Phlox subulate and douglasii varieties
   Polygonum vaccinifolium
   Sedum album 'Coral Carpet'
   Saxifrage encrusted types
   Sempervivum large rosette types
   Thymus citriodorus 'Aureus'
   Thymus drucei in variety
   Veronica cinerea
   Veronica pectinata 'Rosea'

f) **Plants for Wall Crevices**
   Arenaria montana
   Campanula 'Birch Hybrid'
   Campanula portenschlagiana
   Cerastium
   Erinus in variety
   Geranium 'Ballerina'
   Geranium subcaulescens 'Splendens'
   Hypericum polyphyllum Grandiflorum
   Lewisia varieties
   Saponaria ocymoides

g) **Plants for Sinks & Troughs**
   Androsace in variety
   Antennaria, dwarfest varieties
   Armeria caespitosa
   Campanula, dwarfest varieties
   Dianthus, dwarfest varieties
   Draba in variety
   Erinus in variety
   Geranium, dwarfest varieties
   Hypericum, dwarfest varieties
   Phlox douglasii varieties
   Potentilla, dwarfest varieties
   Primula some varieties
   Raoulia, dwarfest varieties
   Saxifraga, dwarfest varieties
   Sedum spathulifolium varieties
   Sempervivum, dwarfest varieties
   Veronica prostrate varieties

Sempervivum

2. MINIATURE SHRUBS

Andromeda polifolia Nana
Berberis buxifolia Nana
Enonymus Emerald and Gold
Enonymus Emarald Gaiety
Fuchsia Tom Thumb
Gautheria procumbens
Genista lydia
Genista hispanica
Heathers dwarf variety
Hebe Carl Teschner
Hebe Iames Stirling
Hebe Pagei
Hebe Rakaiensis
Kalmia angustifolia rubra
Lavander Munstead
Leucothoe Rainbow
Phormium Tom Thumb
Santolina in variety

3. MINIATURE CONIFERS

Chamaecyparis lawsoniana
   Minima Glanca
Chamaecyparis lawsoniana
   Minima Aurea
Chamaecyparis obtusa Nana Aurea
Chamaecyparis obtusa Nana Gracilis
Chamaecyparis obtusa Pygmea
Chamaecyparis Pisifera Benlevard
Juniperus communus Compressa
Iunipers squamata Blue Star
Picea abies Nidiformis
Picea abies Repens
Picea glauca Albertiana Conica
Picea glauca Albertiana Globe
Pinus muga
Thuja occidentalis Danica
Thuja occidentalis Emerald
Thuja occidentalis Rheingold
Thuja occidentalis Sunkist
Thuja orientalis Aurea Nana

Primula

CLAYGATE GARDEN CENTRE Oaken Lane, Claygate, Surrey KT10 0RH. Tel: 081 398 0047
FARNHAM ROYAL GARDEN CENTRE Cedar Cottage, Crown Lane, Farnham Royal, Slough Berkshire SL2 3SG. Tel: 0753 645627
FOLKESTONE GARDEN CENTRE Ingles Meadow, Jointon Road, Folkestone, Kent CT20 2RS. Tel: 0303 58100
HARE HATCH GARDEN CENTRE Floral Mile, Hare Hatch, Twyford, Nr. Reading, Berkshire RG10 9SJ. Tel: 0734 403933
STROUD GARDEN CENTRE Ebley Road, Stonehouse, Gloucestershire GL10 9SJ. Tel: 045 382 3846
SWINDON GARDEN CENTRE Hyde Road, Stratton St. Margaret, Swindon, Wiltshire SN2 6SE. Tel: 0793 822224
WELLINGBOROUGH GARDEN CENTRE Millers Lane, Wellingborough, Northants NN8 2NF. Tel: 0933 273728
CHURCH LAWFORD GARDEN CENTRE Kings Newnham Road, Church Lawford, Rugby , Warwickshire CV23 9EP. Tel; 0203 542319
HAILSHAM GARDEN CENTRE A22 Lower Dicker, Hailsham, East Sussex BN27 4BA. Tel: 0323 844834
OXFORD GARDEN CENTRE Southern By-Pass, South Hinksey, Oxford. Tel: 0865 326066

EDITOR'S FOREWORD

This unique series takes a completely fresh look at the most popular garden and greenhouse plants.

Written by a team of leading specialists, yet suitable for novice and more experienced gardeners alike, the series considers modern uses of the plants, including refreshing ideas for combining them with other garden or greenhouse plants. This should appeal to the more general gardener who, unlike the specialist, does not want to devote a large part of the garden to a particular plant. Many of the planting schemes and modern uses are beautifully illustrated in colour.

The extensive A-Z lists describe in great detail hundreds of the best varieties and species available today.

For the historically-minded, each book opens with a brief history of the subject up to the present day and, as appropriate, looks at the developments by plant breeders.

The books cover all you need to know about growing and propagating. The former embraces such aspects as suitable sites and soils, planting methods, all-year-round care and how to combat pests, diseases and disorders.

Propagation includes raising plants from seeds and by vegetative means, as appropriate.

For each subject there is a society (sometimes more than one), full details of which round off each book.

The plants that make up this series are very popular and examples can be found in many gardens. However, it is hoped that these books will encourage gardeners to try some of the better, or perhaps more unusual, varieties; ensure some stunning plant associations; and result in the plants being grown well.

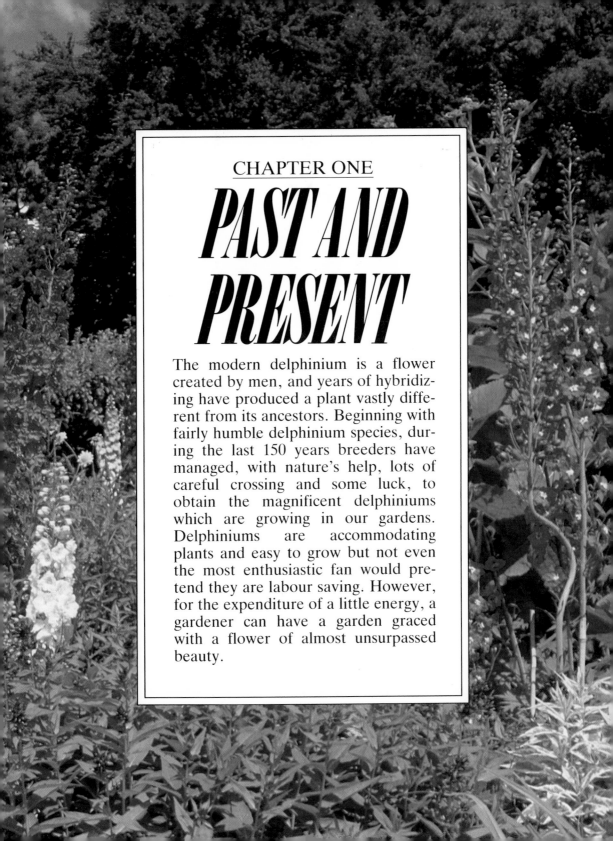

CHAPTER ONE

PAST AND PRESENT

The modern delphinium is a flower created by men, and years of hybridizing have produced a plant vastly different from its ancestors. Beginning with fairly humble delphinium species, during the last 150 years breeders have managed, with nature's help, lots of careful crossing and some luck, to obtain the magnificent delphiniums which are growing in our gardens. Delphiniums are accommodating plants and easy to grow but not even the most enthusiastic fan would pretend they are labour saving. However, for the expenditure of a little energy, a gardener can have a garden graced with a flower of almost unsurpassed beauty.

No one knows for sure which of the many different delphinium species growing worldwide were used by the first delphinium breeders. Most of us tend to think of the delphinium as a typically English garden plant, one that fits into our idyllic picture of a cottage garden where pink roses entwine around the cottage doorway and tall, blue delphiniums dominate the border.

However, as wild flowers they grow in almost every corner of the world except the two Poles and Australia. There are several hundred different species. Amongst others to be found in Africa, there is, growing in Ethiopia, *Delphinium welbeyi* which has bright blue flowers and is scented, while another similar perfumed species, *D. leroyi*, grows on Mount Kilimanjaro. In America, *D. nudicaule* and *D. cardinale* are red delphiniums to be found in California and several others grow high in the Rockies. In Asia there is *D. brunomianum*, a strange purple plant with a musky smell which can be found at 16,000 feet in Tibet; *D. cashmirianum*, not surprisingly, comes from Kashmir and is a short plant with light purple flowers; and the dark blue *D. tatsienense* comes from Szechuan.

Europe, too, has its share with some like *D. staphisagria* growing in the Mediterranean areas, others such as *D. elatum* (possibly one of the foreparents of our present plants) in the Alps, and in Siberia there is *D. grandiflorum*, a superb and easy to raise dwarf plant with dark blue flowers. Ironically, only one delphinium species is said to be indigenous to Britain and, even then, it is more common in other parts of Europe. Furthermore, it was a Frenchman who took the first steps along the path which led to today's beautiful flowers.

EARLY HISTORY

To start at the beginning, the Greeks and the Romans were interested in delphiniums, although for medicinal rather than decorative purposes. The first recorded mention of them was in a work called *Materia Medico* by a Greek called Dioscorides. In it he describes the medical properties of about 600 plants. He mentions two wild delphiniums, one of which, now known as *D. staphisagria*, he prescribes as being good for scorpion bites.

The other delphinium described by Dioscorides was *D. peregrinum* and it is this plant which has given us the name 'delphinium'. According to the Greek botanists, the unopened buds of *D. peregrinum* resembled a small dolphin, or in Latin *delphinium*.

The annual *Consolida ambigua* (*D. ajacis*) may have been the first delphinium to be grown for its beauty as a flower; it was certainly grown in gardens during the reign of the Tudors and Stuarts. It is the one species which grows wild in Great Britain and has a blue flower growing to about 90 cm (3 ft) high. It was called 'Larkes spur' and, not surprisingly, it was the ancestor of our modern annual larkspur.

To the best of our knowledge, the first delphinium hybrid was a chance seedling discovered by a Mr Barlow of Manchester and called *D. barlowii*. The flowers were intense blue and the florets semi-double. The parents were thought to be *D. grandiflorum* and *D. elatum.*

THE FIRST HYBRIDIZERS

The first attempt at intentional crossing began in France when several nursery-men started to produce new varieties, or to use the correct terminology, new cultivars. The most notable was Victor Lemoine whose large nursery at Nancy offered shrubs and hardy plants. Victor Lemoine is believed to have started deliberate crossing in 1848 and the first hybrids were on sale in 1852. It would seem that Lemoine crossed two species, *D. elatum* and *D. formosum*, to obtain his new plants, most of which were semi-double or double. Accordingly, modern day delphiniums are often re-ferred to as elatum delphiniums. Ini-tially, the colours were predominantly shades of blue but gradually the range widened to include combinations of blue with mauve, rose or lilac, sky blue and mauve.

In 1906 Victor Lemoine introduced the delphinium which was to be the forefather of many magnificent delphi-niums. It was called 'Statuaire Rude' and had pale mauve semi-double flow-ers in a magnificent dense floral column. In Britain it caused a minor sensation when exhibited at the Royal Horticul-tural Society Hall in 1908. Victor Le-moine died in 1911 and although his son Emile carried on delphinium raising and, indeed, introduced several new cultivars, others had taken up the quest and were getting better results.

One of these was James Kelway, the founder of the famous nursery at Lang-port, Somerset, who obtained delphi-niums from France and began his own breeding. From 1881 until the late 1920s Kelway introduced scores of new varieties. They brought the delphinium to British gardens. Probably the most famous Kelway introduction was 'King of the Delphiniums'. Its colour was a combination of gentian blue and plum with a white eye while there was 60 cm (2 ft) of flower on the spike.

□ BLACKMORE AND LANGDON

But it was in 1901 that the event which was to change the delphinium for ever took place: Charles Langdon, who had been gardener to the Reverend E. Lascelles, entered into partnership with an innkeeper called James Blackmore to start a nursery to be called Blackmore and Langdon's Nursery. This nursery was to become synonymous with del-phiniums, with the name becoming famous throughout the world.

Oddly enough, it may have been chance that first persuaded the partners to specialize in delphiniums because their first catalogue listed only a few seedlings. Charles Langdon had given a box of delphinium seedlings to A. A. Walters, another Bath nurseryman. Walters was impressed with one of these seedlings, a short semi-double purple-violet with a large white eye. It was named 'Reverend E. Lascelles' and it received an Award of Merit from the Royal Horticultural Society in 1907. This plant is still in existence in some gardens.

In 1907 Blackmore and Langdon listed their own cultivars, using existing plants which they had obtained from Kelways, Victor Lemoine and Mynheer Van Veen, a grower in Holland. The delphiniums used included 'King of the Delphiniums' and 'Statuaire Rude'. They were soon gaining excellent results and many fine varieties were included in their catalogues. In 1919 Royal Horticultural Society Awards of Merits went to 'Millicent Blackmore' and 'Sir Douglas Haig', two delphiniums which have become landmarks in delphinium history. 'Sir Douglas Haig' was a purple with exceptionally large spikes, while 'Millicent Blackmore' had blue and mauve florets 6.5 cm (2½ in) across and a broad-based symmetrical spike. Both had 'Statuaire Rude' as one of their parents.

Blackmore and Langdon became more systematic with their delphinium breeding and more seed raised from hand-crossed seed was used in their programme. Good records were kept and knowledge increased. The prime concern was to breed delphiniums, not for colour or novelty but for their vigour and good constitution. Plants that would be genuine perennials. Charles Langdon was sure if delphiniums were to be a commercial proposition, they had to be plants that would grow and last in anyone's garden. To this end Blackmore and Langdon's regularly raised between 50,000 and 100,000 seedlings a year and success followed success. In the five delphinium trials held between 1925 and 1935, 45 of the 96 awards were gained by Blackmore and Langdon. When one considers that there were as many as 107 other breeders introducing new delphiniums during this time, the achievement is considerable.

In 1924 Blackmore and Langdon introduced 'Lady Eleanor' which was in its way and its time one of the finest delphiniums ever raised. It was sky-blue shaded mauve with a fully double floret. Its constitution has always been excellent and it can still be found growing in one or two gardens. But there were other fine plants, far too numerous to mention, ones like 'Bridesmaid' and 'Tessa', both raised in the 1930s, both silvery-mauve, both still going strong in the 1960s.

Blackmore and Langdon reigned supreme during the period between the two World Wars when delphinium breeding and delphinium growing was at its peak.

□ WATKIN SAMUEL

At this time one of the other more notable series of delphiniums was the so-called Wrexham Hollyhock strain. These were raised by an amateur Watkin Samuel who began breeding delphiniums in 1909 using, it is said, 'Millicent Blackmore' and 'Sir Douglas Haig'. In the twenties he grew about 5000 seedlings a year and in 1921 he caused quite a sensation when, as an unknown amateur, five of his delphiniums gained Awards of Merit at the Royal Horticultural Society show. One of these was 'Cambria', a late flowering mauve and blue plant, which became very popular.

Watkin Samuel's cultivars were sold by Bees of Chester who advertised them

The delphinium 'Conspicuous', red roses and yellow achillea making their presence felt in a mixed border.

as Hollyhock delphiniums. This name implies a feature which was to consign Watkin Samuel's magnificent creations to a blind alley of delphinium evolution. Put simply, they were too tall, often growing up to 3m (10ft) high and making them prone to wind damage. Many were single flowered too, which meant they dropped their petals quickly. Nevertheless, Samuel's delphiniums were widely grown and in the post war years they remained popular. Those who saw the Hollyhock delphiniums growing well have never forgotten them.

□ FRANK REINELT

Watkin Samuel sold large quantities of seed to the United States where a hybridizer who was pursuing a different path in delphinium breeding certainly purchased a packet or two. The man was Frank Reinelt, a Czech who had emigrated to California in 1925. His objective was to raise a seed strain that would come true to colour from seed, so that if someone wanted to grow, say, purple delphiniums, they could buy a packet of purple-flowered seed and know they would get just that. In normal circumstances delphiniums do not come true from seed. Unlike Blackmore and Langdon, who concentrated on constitution and perenniality, Frank Reinelt had no interest in long-lived delphiniums because the weather in California called for a different routine. There, in warmer conditions, delphiniums grow the whole year round, often flowering themselves to death. Accordingly, the United States market re-

quired a seed strain which enabled gardeners to sow in mid to late autumn and to get flowers in mid-spring, with repeat flowers in early/mid summer and yet another in early autumn. The United Kingdom type of delphinium growing with long-lived cultivars and propagation by taking cuttings is simply unworkable there.

To achieve his aim Frank Reinelt used a method called line breeding where he took the best two plants in the colour he required and crossed them with each other. From their offspring he selected the best one, i.e. the one closest to the colour required with the nicest florets and spike, and self fertilized it. All the rejected seedlings were thrown out. In the third year he would select the best two seedlings and cross them. In this way he gradually eliminated the variations and obtained a selection of plants which would give seed true in colour and form. The seed was marketed and sold as Giant Pacific hybrids.

By itself, line breeding to produce true seed strains was nothing new – seed companies had been doing it for years – but Frank Reinelt was to change the course of delphinium breeding in another way. He had an ambition and that was to obtain a red delphinium. In California there are two wild delphinium species which are red. *D. nudicaule* is short growing with vermilion scarlet flowers, while *D. cardinale* is a taller, scarlet-flowered plant which looks a little like a normal garden delphinium. It was the latter which Frank decided to use; he reasoned that if he could cross _D. cardinale_ with one of the Giant Pacific hybrids he should get a red version of the garden delphinium. Unfortunately, _D. cardinale_ has 16 chromosomes whereas elatum delphiniums have 32, which means they will not cross naturally. Very occasionally _D. cardinale_ will have double chromosomes but Frank Reinelt decided to double them using X-rays. This he did and managed to obtain plants which would cross with elatum delphiniums and set seed. The attempt was a failure in one respect but a glorious triumph in another, for the red delphinium never materialized but the seedlings which Reinelt did obtain had a brightness and clearness of colour which had not been seen previously. He now produced rich purples and clear bright blues. Once again the way the delphinium was going had changed but there were to be repercussions. _D. cardinale_ is a short-lived plant and its hybrid offspring tended to be short-lived too. This, of course, did not worry Frank Reinelt who was not interested in perennial delphiniums but it has had its effects on the British delphinium.

□ FRANK BISHOP

In 1930 a man named Frank Bishop joined the British Delphinium Society. Frank was a mason from Windsor and, perhaps as a result of his professional training, he had a certain methodical approach. In 1929 he had visited the British Delphinium Society show and had been entranced by the sight of the ranks of delphiniums. He decided to specialize in them. Carefully studying the delphinium requirements he worked away, until after a preliminary attempt the previous year, he entered the British Delphinium Society show of 1933 and carried away a dozen prizes. As A. G. L. Hellyer wrote at the time, 'At last the amateur has learned to emulate the trade grower, and, be it whispered, occasionally beat him at his own game'. These were prophetic words.

Frank Bishop had become interested in breeding and received awards in 1934, 1935, 1937 and 1938. It seems that from the first he had a clear aim, to grow pure blue cultivars. He believed that the few semi-double blue delphiniums available were inferior in all respects to those of other colours. Using existing British cultivars he had by 1939 raised several seedlings which ranged from pale sky blue to gentian, although they still had a distinct mauve flush.

In 1940 he bought Giant Pacific seed from Vetterle and Reinelt; this was from the 'Blue Jay' series which produced a plant with intense dark blue flowers and a black eye. Frank Bishop liked the colour and size of florets on the 'Blue Jay' seedlings he obtained but thought the spike gappy and ill-formed. He crossed the best of these seedlings with the best of his own seedlings. It was not long before he obtained interesting results, plants such as 'Mrs Frank Bishop' a lovely gentian blue, 'Agnes Brook' cornflower blue and 'Harvest Moon' a silvery-blue.

In 1947 Baker's Nurseries offered Frank Bishop the opportunity to work on his delphiniums full time and he eventually moved to Codsall where the

A beautiful mixture of plant shapes and foliage types with delphiniums providing rich colour.

nursery was situated. More fine delphiniums resulted, including several which were not blue but which proved most influential: 'Swanlake', a white with a black eye, attracted a great deal of attention; 'Cinderella', a superb short heliotrope; and the violet 'Minstrel Boy'.

Soon after his move to Baker's, Frank noticed a seedling with perfect 10cm (4in) florets, although the spike itself was not that good. He crossed this seedling with a vigorous, mildew resistant blue seedling that had a heavy well-built spike. Nothing worthwhile turned up in the first generation of seedlings. However, he self-crossed the best. The next generation produced a plant with a good spike but the florets were not large. He persisted and selfed this seedling to obtain about 100 plants. At last he had succeeded, for when the seedlings flowered one stood out. It was, as Frank Bishop noted, an 'exceptionally vigorous plant with a grand spike with florets measuring 4 inches (10cm) at the base, 3½ inches (9cm) at the top'.

This plant was called 'Great Britain' and from it Frank Bishop aimed to raise a new strain he called the Commonwealth strain. Regrettably, Frank Bishop died in 1957 and although a number of Commonwealth cultivars were released, their full potential was never exploited. 'Great Britain' itself did not perform well in all gardens and indeed, was never widely grown.

It is disappointing to think of Frank Bishop's dream petering out so, but he had changed the direction of delphinium evolution. He had succeeded in marrying the bright colours of Frank Reinelt's Giant Pacific hybrids with the floret size and better form of the British delphinium. But, ironically, the most famous Bishop delphinium was not spotted by Frank Bishop.

□ ENTER THE AMATEURS

Ronald Parrett, an accountant working for Beaverbrook Newspapers, had become interested in delphiniums and in 1947 he purchased a packet of Bishop seed which Baker's Nurseries had just started to sell. He raised 36 seedlings, one of which was large flowered with a good spike. Its outstanding feature was its colour, a very pure sky blue. In 1949 Ronald Parrett entered the British Delphinium Society show and the seedling won the Best Seedling class, a feat repeated in 1950 and 1951. It was then named 'Daily Express' and was purchased and grown by many people. Its constitution was excellent, being completely perennial, a feature not always found in Bishop cultivars because of their Giant Pacific parentage.

This chance seedling had many repercussions in the delphinium world, not least that it pushed Ronald Parrett into the forefront of the British Delphinium Society. He had a gift for publicity and membership of the Society soared and interest in delphiniums increased. It was a heyday for delphinium growing, perhaps not as great as pre-war days for the situation had changed – the days of great wealth and large gardens had gone. Instead there were small gardens and the keen amateur. These were the golden years of Frank Bishop, Frank Reinelt and Blackmore and Langdon at their peak.

But it was a turning point. A turning point heralded by Ronald Parrett himself: the amateur breeder was about to come into his own. There had always been keen amateur raisers but the professional nurserymen had dominated. From the time Ronald Parrett came on the scene the influence of amateur breeders gradually increased until eventually there were no professional breeders. Not least of Ronald Parrett's contributions to the amateur was his book *Delphiniums* published in 1961. This, the best of all books about delphiniums, not only persuaded many people to grow delphiniums, it influenced the views of several would-be raisers.

□ BLACKMORE AND LANGDON AFTER THE WAR

However, this is to jump ahead. Following the war the major influence on British delphinium growing was Blackmore and Langdon. Continuing where they had left off in 1939 they produced a string of notable delphiniums, a list so long that it is impossible to do justice to their achievements. Even to pick out a few influential cultivars from so many introduced is difficult and makes the lists very subjective. 'Silver Moon' was for me a landmark not because of its colour – bright mauve and a white eye – but because of its form, which is broad at the base tapering upwards; and its constitution, which is healthy, mildew-free and perennial. I recall thinking it the 'Peace' of the delphinium world. It

is still in the Wisley trials but it is not the plant that I remember in my mind's eye. 'Fanfare' was, and still is, a favourite with many people. Again, it is silvery mauve and it usually flowers early.

Light mauves were a Blackmore and Langdon speciality and they raised many more fine plants in this colour but they reigned supreme in the purple shades too, with plants like 'Guy Langdon', a plum purple-flowered cultivar with a massive spike which won dozens of first prizes on the show bench. Oddly enough Blackmore and Langdon did not list 'Guy Langdon' in their catalogue for very long, but for years after leading amateurs continued to grow and propagate it, because of its exhibition potential.

'Purple Triumph' was a beautiful delphinium, deep violet purple in colour, and tall and stately in form; 'Emir' was shorter but had large florets of purple with a large white and purple striped eye. A plant that impressed everyone at the Chelsea Flower Show when it was first shown was 'Chelsea Star', an absolutely beautiful rich velvet purple with a white eye. It is still widely grown simply because of its colour, which no breeder has succeeded in repeating in a better plant. Unfortunately, 'Chelsea Star' is prone to mildew and can have gappy spikes. A delphinium should have florets which just touch or only slightly overlap so that the stem cannot be seen. A gappy spike is one where the opposite has happened and there are gaps separating the florets.

Blackmore and Langdon's entry into the field of blue delphiniums was comparatively late but in 1959 they introduced 'Greville Stevens' and 'Molly Buchanan'. I recall seeing 'Greville Stevens' for the first time and being bowled over by its beautiful bright gentian blue colour, nicely set off by a white eye, 'Molly Buchanan' was a deep gentian but had a black eye and was, perhaps, slightly overshadowed by 'Greville Stevens' at the time, but she had a role to play later on.

Two years later came, arguably, the most beautiful blue delphinium of them all, 'Blue Nile'. The colour was outstanding, pure mid-blue with a white eye. Its form was good and it was perennial, although unfortunately not in all gardens, for I must confess I never had any luck with it. But other people did, and grown well it can be breathtaking.

Another superb plant that has stood the test of time is 'Fenella' which has a gentian blue floret with a black eye, and which seems to come good each season.

Other colours came too: 'Butterball' and 'Sungleam', cream cultivars; and 'Strawberry Fair', a rich mulberry rose. The flow seemed endless.

Sadly, in 1978 Blackmore and Langdon announced that due to high costs and falling sales they had ceased hybridizing, although they would continue to sell delphiniums. The decision, though understandable was, to say the least, a tragedy for all delphinium lovers.

THE PRESENT

It was now up to the amateur breeders for there was no professional hybridizing being undertaken. The Delphinium Society determined that the delphinium would not decline and urged its members to raise new cultivars.

One member, a keen grower, had already shown the way. Growing delphiniums in a small-scale garden in Ealing where the soil was, as he put it, 'London dirt', Tom Cowan had raised several outstanding plants: 'Spindrift' and 'Gossamer', and most importantly 'Loch Nevis' and 'Loch Leven'. These latter two were sister plants coming from the same cross with one parent, 'Molly Buchanan'. The two sisters are somewhat similar, both being light blue with a white eye. However, 'Loch Nevis' is taller and forms large pyramidal spikes and was an outstanding exhibition plant which won scores of first prizes, although unfortunately it now appears to be deteriorating and is sometimes a shadow of what it used to be. 'Loch Leven' is shorter and well proportioned and it can win prizes at shows; it is also still growing well. This deterioration does happen with plants, even shrubby ones like roses, probably because they have been continually propagated.

Others have followed Tom Cowan: men like Roy Latty, whose knowledge of and concern for delphiniums is unsurpassed, and who has raised a number of excellent cultivars including 'Sandpiper' a really good white with a black eye.

David Bassett started raising delphiniums in the late 1970s but already he is on his way to becoming the foremost amateur raiser of all time. David, a winner at many Delphinium Society shows, has a meticulous approach to

White delphiniums can lighten a border and make a contrast for brighter plants.

breeding which is reflected in the neat and tidy appearance of his delphiniums. His first introduction was 'Emily Hawkins', a light blue with a fawn eye, but 'Rosemary Brock' is proving to be an outstanding pink.

Occasionally a plant comes along which seems to take all the prizes at the shows. Such a plant is the purple 'Bruce', raised by Duncan McGlashan, yet another knowledgeable and enthusiastic amateur raiser. He has since followed this early success with a number of exciting new cultivars.

Other amateurs, many of whom deserve mentioning if there was space, have done their part and have bred some magnificent delphiniums.

Since 1978 there has been a problem because there has not been a retail outlet for delphiniums other than Blackmore and Langdon. Garden centres have been content to sell delphiniums raised from seed. This is understandable because taking the necessary delphinium cuttings is a labour intensive and skilled task. The result has been that although there have been good new cultivars in existence, the average gardener has not been able to buy them because they were not readily available.

Thankfully this has changed recently and there are now four nurseries specializing in delphiniums. Two of them are raising new delphinium cultivars: Woodfield Brothers have introduced several, including one, 'Clifford Pink', which looks to be a plant of the future; Butterfield's Nurseries have been working with a leading amateur raiser Colin Edwards and they, also, have a number of fine cultivars including 'Claire' which won an Award of Merit in the 1987 delphinium trials at Wisley.

THE FUTURE

What of the future? Who can say, but there is one man who may have a great influence on the likely appearance of delphiniums in the year 2000 and that is Bob Legro, the raiser of the red delphiniums which have attracted so much attention recently.

Dr Robert Legro, a Dutch professor, began his work in 1953 by trying to cross the red wild species with the modern elatum delphinium. He crossed *D. nudicaule* first of all, a short bushy orange-red plant, with *D. cardinale*, a taller scarlet plant, to produce a hybrid with features somewhere between the two. Using chemical means, he crossed some of these hybrids with an elatum delphinium. In 1962, he eventually obtained plants which had orange-pink semi-double florets, and with a branching habit. Bob Legro realized he had some way to go before he had cultivars to match the normal delphinium. Work continued and the plants have steadily improved, the stems have lengthened and the floret size increased. Called University hybrids, because the work had begun at Wageningen University, the plants were shown to the public during the 1988 Chelsea Flower Show. Much interest was shown and it is hoped that, eventually, they will be growing in our gardens.

CHAPTER TWO

PLANTING IDEAS

It is concerning that sometimes our views about delphiniums can be so stereotyped, for example that they are cottage garden plants or that they are not suitable for small gardens. It is such a pity because delphiniums are quite versatile; and besides which, why should the fellows with the large gardens in the country grow all the best plants? A few ideas and a little thought in planning the planting of delphiniums can do wonders in any situation. They have much to offer: wonderful colours, beautiful florets, and an eye-catching form. With such attributes it is almost a crime not to have delphiniums in the garden.

THE DELPHINIUM COLOUR

The colour spectrum of the delphinium is large, ranging through white, cream, pink, mauve, blue, violet and purple; all cool shades, rich, yet without being garish. For me the blue is the prime attraction and the modern delphinium covers most of the shades of blue: sky blue, mid blue and deep blue, the only missing hue being turquoise, and that will come one day. Blue is not a common colour in garden plants and the delphinium blue is really special, particularly in the garden when it reflects the clear blue of a beautiful summer sky. Very pleasing effects can be created by using complementary colours such as groups of *Geranium* 'Johnson's Blue'

and *Salvia superba* 'East Friesland' planted close to a few blue delphiniums, perhaps the slate blue 'Gillian Dallas' or the shorter mid-blue 'Loch Leven'. Another possibility could be *Leucanthemum maximum* (formerly *Chrysanthemum maximum*) 'H. Siebert', (a single variety worth looking around for), white *Astilbe* 'Deutschland' and *Achillea* 'White Pearl' (a plant which can be invasive), combined with the white delphinium 'Moonbeam' or, better still, 'Demavand'. However, some very effective results can be gained by taking a bold approach with a group of yellow plants, for example: *Achillea* 'Moonshine' or *Alchemilla mollis* contrasting with blue delphiniums, or instead of using white delphiniums with the white

1. *Contrasting flower shapes, with the tall delphiniums offset by the flat heads of the achillea (foreground right & background left).*

perennials as mentioned previously, planting instead the dark blue 'Fenella'. But one has to be wary of creating something too garish. A slightly more subtle approach might be to use softer tones such as a group of the lovely blue delphinium 'Skyline' as a companion to the beautiful white cluster-flowered rose 'Margaret Merrill'. The possibilities are endless and, undoubtedly, with just a little thought a dull or awkward corner can be brightened up, or a sunny spot made to create a veritable feast of colour.

THE DELPHINIUM SHAPE

The shape of a delphinium plant is impressive, for it is upright and tall which means it is able to make its presence felt. In the same way that Nelson's column in Trafalgar Square will always cause you to look upwards, so the delphinium columns lead your eyes skywards, giving additional dimension to a border (Fig. 1). A good delphinium plant will catch the eye, and even a small group will dominate, but in a subtle rather than a loud way. The plant can be viewed all round with equal pleasure and looks good from a distance and absolutely wonderful close up. Tall spikes look dramatic but overdone their impact can be lost. As with most things in life moderation is better and a rounded shape nearby heightens the effect, for example the columns of a nice group of blue 'Emily Hawkins' delphiniums could be balanced by a group of pink phlox to lessen the overwhelming impact.

2. Contrasting foliage with the oval, fleshy, leaved hosta and the upright iris set against the finely-cut delphinium leaves.

THE DELPHINIUM FOLIAGE

There is nothing wonderful about delphinium foliage; it is a pleasant enough colour with a finely cut leaf and there is usually quite a bit of it. However, it does give another degree of foliage texture in your border and provides a setting for the more interesting foliage plants such as hostas, irises and hemerocallis (Fig. 2). Foliage can give additional interest to a border and it never fails to surprise me how the day lilies in my garden give a luxuriant, almost tropical look as they throw new growth in the spring. There is another aspect with regard to colour, where grey plants

such as artemisia – silvery grey as *Stachys lanata* or purple like *Salvia officinalis* 'Purpurascens' (the purple sage which is enjoyed by bees and butterflies) – can contrast with the light green of delphiniums.

Light blue belladonna delphiniums make a dainty group and provide material for flower arranging too.

EXTENDING THE SEASON

The flowering season of a delphinium is not long (although longer than a peony or a bearded iris), but can be extended fairly easily. Some cultivars flower as early as mid-June (early summer) in favoured spots in southern England, while others will not start until July mid-summer. 'Spindrift' and 'De-mavand' are always early in my garden whereas 'Skyline' and 'Hilda Lucas' are late, often starting to flower four weeks after the first. This means that a group of each will give a longer period when there is good colour. The flower side-shoots called laterals also bloom later than the main flower spike. It is prefer-able to trim some of the top ones off to enable the flower spike to be seen at its best. This improves the laterals because they become larger, and if, when the main spike has finished flowering, it is cut off, the laterals will bloom and give another two weeks of colour.

Seedlings that are sown in early spring will flower in early autumn, and, again, help to increase the season of delphinium flower.

USING DELPHINIUMS TO GOOD EFFECT

All the experts say that a group of plants looks better than a border full of solitary plants and this is particularly true in the case of delphiniums which look very isolated on their own in a border. A minimum of three plants is required if anything like a good effect is to be created. I would go a little further and suggest that these should be of the same cultivar because it produces a bolder effect. Clearly with smaller plants even more are required if they are to show up. *D. nudicaule* is a small plant with orange-red flowers which is pretty but not particularly significant. On its own it is lost but a group of six or more of them and it becomes a stronger focal point, and still does not take up much room.

Having said this, most keen gardeners are squirrels when it comes to collecting plants for their garden. They scrounge a cutting from a friend here and buy a mystery specimen from a plant sale there. In my own case, this became a problem as more of my garden became a hotch potch of isolated plants in all shapes and sizes. I now have a 'nursery' which is a small patch where I put these plants to try them out and to build up the numbers either by cuttings or division.

It is usual in a border to have the tall plants at the back and then to gradually size them with the short ones at the front, giving a tiered effect. This is only sensible, as no one would want a small choice plant hidden by a 1.8m (6ft) delphinium. However, if this kind of planting is carried out to the letter the overall result can look artificial. Some taller plants should be brought nearer to the front. The way to do this is by having a group of, say, delphiniums coming forward in a triangle so that the base with most delphiniums are at the back but some at the front. If mixed cultivars are being used then one or two shorter ones could be in the forefront.

Another factor to bear in mind is the flowering season. It is quite reasonable and very sensible to have a taller later flowering plant in front of a shorter early flowering one, so as one dies down, the other comes into flower and hides the remains which are often not always terribly beautiful. Delphiniums can look a bit of a mess after flowering and could well be one of those plants to hide – lupins are most certainly another.

DELPHINIUM REQUIREMENTS

The first consideration when planting is whether the position is suitable for the plant. So many people try to fit the plants to unsuitable sites and are then disappointed. In the case of the delphinium it will not tolerate shade, and the rule is to choose a spot that is in sun for at least half the day. One cross delphiniums have had to bear over the years is that because they are tall plants, they tend to get stuck at the back of the border, possibly next to a wall or a hedge. The problem here is that they require plenty of water and such places tend to be dry and, what is more, probably short of nutrients, especially when the site is close to a hedge. When choosing a position for delphiniums remember they need light, water and food. It makes sense when you realize that the shoots come through in late winter/early spring and by the end of early summer they will have had to make 1.5–1.8 m (5–6 ft) of growth and produce a multi-flowered spike. They cannot do this on a starvation diet.

Oddly enough the type of soil counts for very little. They will grow happily in sandy soils, clay or chalky ones, *provided* there is *plenty* of humus and that the site does not get waterlogged in winter.

SETTINGS FOR DELPHINIUMS

The elatum delphinium will look good in most gardens and, if we include all types of delphinium, I cannot think of any type of garden that they will not look well in. The setting for them can be almost what you choose, or more realistically what you have available. Those lucky people who live in lovely old houses and cottages with mellowed brick, Cotswold or Yorkshire stone, have the ideal setting and will find the delphinium complementing the building wonderfully. Those of us who live in semi-detached houses built in the thirties or those with really modern houses have not such a perfect setting but can plant delphiniums that will soften the outline and embellish the sometimes unlovely look of the building. Obviously, some colour combinations will need to be avoided; for example if the house

is made of bright red brick the blues, purples and whites should be chosen rather than the pink and mauve shades.

I must admit I do not see colour clashes with the buildings as much of a problem. To my way of thinking the major difficulty with the small modern garden is trying to avoid it looking like an enclosure – all fence and house – giving a feeling of claustrophobia. The aim should be, I believe, to make it seem larger than it is by hiding the fences and having hidden places of interest, hopefully making the garden seem part of something far bigger and not just a hemmed-in space. Easier said than done, as many of us have found. But, use of shrubs, trees, hedges and climbers can provide the basic framework and clothe the bare fences and boundary walls. A darkish hedge or even a screen of ivy can set off the light blue or any of the lighter coloured delphinium spikes wonderfully.

Having talked about hiding the boundary walls, I must admit that a nice wall can be a very good backdrop for delphiniums, but I suspect that nice walls are not to be found in too many recently established gardens.

Generally, delphiniums can be a great help in trying to achieve the kind of 'secret garden' effect; because they are tall they can add a sense of height without filling masses of space and with the judicious use of the shorter cultivars quite an optical illusion of distance can be achieved; they can create a temporary curtain to hide another feature and, best of all, they can bring a great deal of rich colour into a small space at an important time of the year.

One snag is that delphiniums are transitory; there is nothing at all showing in winter and very little after they have finished flowering, and ideally a garden should have interest all the year round. Delphiniums should therefore be regarded as a decoration, the jewel in the crown during summer, but even so there are a host of ways they can be used to make a garden very special.

DELPHINIUMS IN THE GARDEN

When starting their gardens some organized people sit down with paper and pencil and draw out careful plans setting out just which plants they will have in it. Some get a garden design firm in to construct the garden for them. Others start with a few paths and the odd bit of lawn and then cadge and buy plants to gradually fill the spaces. The majority of us move into a house with an existing garden which we gradually change to our liking. As I have already mentioned I am, regrettably, of the bits and pieces school of gardening, often acquiring a plant and then searching the garden for a space to put it. This is quite wrong and I ought to be ashamed of myself. I have drawn up a hundred plans for my small garden and not achieved a quarter of what I visualized.

It's a bit difficult to keep to plans anyway. Firstly, gardens are a living thing and plants frequently have a will of their own, either growing bigger than you had wanted or not liking the 'ideal' position you had chosen for them. Secondly, they are ongoing things and they evolve from year to year as we try to improve them. I find I am learning every day and it amazes me how many times friends introduce me to plants I have not seen before. There is no doubt in my mind that studying other people's gardens is the best way to get ideas of your own. It seems to me therefore, that a flexible approach to planning is required all the time. Sometimes a combination which seemed ideal on paper looks hideous in reality. Equally, another time a happy mishap throws two plants together and they make absolutely first-class companions. Thirdly and most importantly, gardens are individual things. They are yours, reflecting your taste, your likes and dislikes. I am very wary of garden 'experts' who say that you must do this or you must do that. Opinions differ, even between husbands and wives, over what looks good in a garden. I like my delphiniums and if my garden were only 3m (10ft) square I would still grow a few, regardless of the fact they may look out of proportion.

One of the dilemmas in planning is whether to try to have colour throughout the year or whether to aim for a series of peak flowering periods. Personally, I feel that if by some means you could even the flowering so that each month had much the same proportion of colour, it probably would not amount to a lot in most of our gardens. I think it is easier to be realistic and to plan for, say, three peak periods and be reconciled to the fact that during those 'in-between' moments there will not be a lot of colour apart from conifers and foliage plants to make the garden look reasonable. At the end of early summer, the commencement of delphinium flowering time, is a period when there are limitless possibilities for a good splash of colour. Achillea, alstroemeria, astilbe, campanula, erigeron, hemerocallis, *Lychnis chalcedonica*, lythrum, *Monarda didyma*, penstemon, scabious, sidalcea and verbascum, to name but a few, are all in flower. The most novice gardener could be sure of a fine display with a selection to choose from like that. But how does he or she use them?

THE MIXED BORDER

Herbaceous borders are beautiful features. Set against the background of a 1.8 m (6 ft) wall or hedge, usually yew (which, incidentally, is an ideal backcloth for light blue delphiniums), large groups of herbaceous plants are grown in splendour. Technically an herbaceous plant is one that does not form a persistent woody stem, but it is more commonly understood to be perennials which die down in autumn and reappear the following spring. One of the prime requisites of the traditional herbaceous border is space, for to look effective it has to be a good length and at least 2.7 m (9 ft) wide – great if you own a stately home with large grounds but not so good if you have a modern garden where there simply is not room. The mixed border is one solution. Rather like the cottage garden, there are no firm rules and it does give the opportunity to choose from any of the wide range of plants and shrubs now available. Shrubs and roses will provide the basic framework; even conifers and heathers can be effective if used sensibly. In fact mixed borders give you the opportunity to grow what you will and if you like, to cheat like mad and to have colour throughout the year by filling in with annuals or by growing plants in pots and putting them in gaps that have appeared. I plant daffodils and tulips in large pots in late summer and early autumn and then bury them, pots and all, so that they can be lifted the moment flowering has finished. This allows the bulbs to remain undisturbed while in the border there are no clumps of unsightly leaves withering away as the early summer plants flower. This method also gives the opportunity to get a good display from an area of heavy soil which doesn't seem to favour anything. Such an area can look really good if the tops of the pots are covered with peat. The bad news is that this kind of treatment does nothing for the pots, so use old ones.

DELPHINIUM COMPANIONS

Delphiniums are traditionally one of the stock items of the herbaceous border. Along with lupins, phlox and Michaelmas daisies, three other main stays, they help to provide colour from late spring to mid-autumn. The start of the delphinium flowering comes in the middle of the lupin season and they look delightful together. The start of the phlox season commences as the delphiniums finish, while the Michaelmas daisy flowering comes at a time when the delphinium seedlings raised from seed sown in early spring are giving their first flowers. There is still a place for lupins, phlox and Michaelmas daisies and, naturally, delphiniums, in the mixed border. A flower I would add to this little list of 'main stays' is hemerocallis, better known as day lilies, which are superb plants for the border; their rush-like foliage has real architectural value and although, as the name implies, the flowers only last a short while, they have plenty and are in flower for a long period, usually commencing in the middle of the delphinium season. The principal colours are yellow and mahogany red and the yellow goes quite nicely with the delphinium blue.

□ THE LUPIN

Lupins are easy to grow although they cannot stand chalky soil and dislike applications of lime. Their requirements are totally different from the delphinium but they seem to go together. I remember some years ago I had a nice little collection of Russell lupins. In an excess of enthusiasm I treated them like my delphiniums, mulching them with manure and giving them gallons of liquid feed. The following winter most of them disappeared. My soil is of a clayey nature but that does not seem to worry them; however, too much manure makes for lush growth which causes them to rot away. You can still buy named Russell lupins but some varieties are getting very old and are riddled with virus; several are ones that came from the famous allotment where George Russell originally raised them half a century ago. To the best of my knowledge only one nursery is currently raising new Russell lupin cultivars. I raise my plants from seed, an easy process provided the hard seed case is chipped, and far cheaper.

If you have the space it is preferable to raise them in a nursery bed so that the colour can be seen before putting them out into the borders. With a bit of luck you will get some of the yellow shades which go beautifully with the blue delphiniums. *L. arboreus* (the tree lupin) can look well with delphiniums, although it is rather short lived. It grows about 60–120 cm (2–4 ft) high, with a similar spread, and has small yellow flowers.

Possibly the major objection to lupins is the short flowering season and the look of the plants following flowering. Treating them as a biennial can solve the problem, sowing the seed in mid-spring and then keeping them in a nursery bed until ready to plant out in autumn. The following season, once they have finished flowering they can be dug out and annuals planted in their place. Drastic action maybe, but it does mean not losing out on lupins and still having plenty of colour later in the season.

□ THE PHLOX

Phlox require more or less the same conditions as delphiniums in that they prefer rich soil with plenty of moisture. They do not respond to good treatment like delphiniums but if you do keep them well watered you will be surprised how much better they will be compared with the yellow twisted specimens in less well cared for gardens.

Rather like the Russell lupins, the cultivars available are not as good as they were. In the 1950s Baker's of Codsall, who marketed the Russell lupins, also sold phlox raised by Captain B. H. Symons Jeune. His phlox were superior to any others but when he died his work discontinued. There are still Symons Jeune phlox being sold but the stock has deteriorated. Occasionally, a new phlox cultivar appears but to my prejudiced eyes they aren't up to those raised forty years ago. However, they are all we have and certainly better than not having any. For me there is nothing quite like sitting in the garden on a warm summer evening with the scent of phlox in the air.

Phlox can be prone to eelworm and it pays to replenish your stock frequently by taking root cuttings and planting them in a new site.

□ THE MICHAELMAS DAISY

For some reason Michaelmas daisies are not as popular as they were, presumably because they get mildew and can be straggly. As with the phlox I cannot imagine a garden without them. In early autumn they provide lots of colour and as an additional bonus, together with *Sedum spectabile*, they attract tortoise shell and peacock butterflies. It may seem strange to include them in a delphinium book but, as mentioned previously, if delphinium seed is sown in early spring the seedlings will be in

flower for the first time when the Michaelmas daisies are out, and while the delphinium spikes are not truly representative, they look most attractive together. After several years of having these late-flowering delphinium seedlings, they have become part of my image of autumn along with the Michaelmas daisies, sedum, chrysanthemums and dahlias and, of course, the butterflies. As for the mildew, I am sure it is due to a degree of neglect. Michaelmas daisies are so easy that they never get fed and, as for being watered, who has ever seen anyone watering them? My experience with delphiniums has convinced me that mid to late summer can be dry even in, what seem to be, bad summers. The skies remain cloudy and overcast all day but sometimes very little rain falls. A good soaking with the hose on occasions will do the Michaelmas daisies the world of good. If a garden seems to be prone to mildew, and some certainly are, try *Aster novae-angliae*, which does not seem to suffer as badly, in preference to *A. novi-belgii*. There are many fine asters in the family and certainly every garden should try to include *A. × frikartii* and *A. amellus*.

□ THE ROSE

Roses and delphiniums make one of the most pleasing combinations in the garden world. The magic goes beyond the fact that they flower at more or less the same time in early summer. I suspect it is because the colours blend so well, the soft pinks and apricot shades of the roses, with the blue hues of the delphinium. Occasionally, the rather brash

The new delphinium 'Rosemary Brock', complemented by yellow Lysimachia punctata, *growing at Temple Newsom, Leeds.*

colours of some modern floribundas do not work quite so well. On the other hand many shrub roses, which are becoming increasingly popular, look as though they were made to be grown with delphiniums. The poor shape of hybrid tea bushes tends to discount them in the mixed border but even a single shrub rose can be most successful. They can make large bushes: 'Buff Beauty', for example, an old favourite which in time becomes rather big for a very small garden. 'Penelope', a lovely shell pink, will also grow quite large but can be contained with judicious pruning. As a side issue, I sometimes wonder if we worry too much about size because it often takes a very long time for plants to get to their full size, and anyway we can always trim them back. A pillar rose at the back of the mixed border can add height, and one like 'Compassion' sets off delphiniums beautifully.

Roses look excellent with delphiniums even when not grown in close conjunction; the sight of a group of delphiniums through an arch with rambler 'Albertine' growing upon it is particularly attractive; or delphiniums growing in the garden of a house which has the ancient but still full-of-life ivory rambler 'Félicité et Perpétue' trained up its walls.

□ OTHER PLANTS

The choice of plants which come into bloom at the end of early summer, when the delphiniums flower, is lengthy. The possibilities for happy combinations are many and growers often find out just how successful they are by trial and error or by pure chance. There are quite a number of yellow flowering plants during this period and one tends to think that blue and yellow go together well. Some combinations seem obvious but are not to everybody's taste, for example *Achillea* 'Gold Plate', growing 1.2 m (4 ft) tall with its large flat heads of tiny mustard yellow flowers, might seem a natural with the contrasting spires of deep blue delphiniums, but it is, in my opinion, rather over the top. Anyway, I prefer *Achillea* 'Coronation Gold' which is smaller. The softer lemon-yellow of *Anthemis tinctoria* 'E. C. Buxton' makes an even better contrast. It is not a long-lived plant but is worth persevering with. *Inula orientalis* is well worth looking out for; it has large daisy-like flowers with thin fine petals. The larger *Inula magnifica* is a spectacular plant that needs a large amount of space. A wonderful plant, though perhaps not obviously a companion for delphiniums, is *Coreopsis verticillata* 'Grandiflora' which has ferny foliage and small yellow star-shaped flowers. I must also mention alstroemeria which can be hard to get established and, then, if you want to get rid of it, the very devil to remove. It has lily-like flowers which are set in clusters on the top of leafy stems. Ligtu hybrids are most usually grown and they have pink or orange flowers which go quite nicely with delphiniums. *Alstroemeria aurantiaca* is a showy plant and the hardiest of the genus; growing about 90 cm (3 ft) high, it has bright yellow to orange flowers. *Monarda didyma* 'Cambridge Scarlet' makes a fine contrast to white delphiniums, although the old variety 'Croftway's Pink' does not look bad either. *Campanula persicifolia* is another plant to try with them too.

The best part of having a mixed border is trying everything. The ordinary geraniums which so many of us grow from seed are extremly useful. They can be just the job for filling in that nasty space left by a plant which failed to survive the winter and if they are large enough and not too gaudy they go well with delphiniums and indeed make a bold contrast with the white cultivars.

In a mixed border annuals can play an important role, not only by providing colour but by filling spaces also. Even the best laid plans go astray and plants die, leaving gaps. Spaces are to be avoided at all costs because Nature hates a void and will fill it with weeds. Half-hardy and hardy annuals are better than weeds. Some types of delphiniums are best grown as annuals. A small group of *D. grandiflorum* 'Blue Butterfly' makes an eye-catching patch of bright blue, and even the small red *D. nudicaule* can be effective over a surprisingly long period if planted in a close grouping. The annual larkspur is not to be seen growing in many gardens, which is a shame for it too can make a nice colourful display and you can choose whether to have the tall imperial strain at 90-150cm (3-5ft) or the dwarf rocket strain at 38cm (15in). It is usually recommended that larkspur are sown *in situ*. I find this a bit hit and miss with them coming up in a crowd in one place and none in another. They dislike being transplanted or pricked out so I sow a pinch of seed into a number of pots and place them in the greenhouse. No heat is required and they germinate easily. They are not touched except to thin out a few and when they have gained a reasonable size I put them in their correct positions in the border, taking care not to disturb them or the compost they are growing in.

THE CHEAP BORDER

Buying a collection of hardy plants is expensive and, at the time of writing, a named delphinium will cost you £3. Like most things in life you get what you pay for and if you want the very best then you will have to pay. Nevertheless, most of the hardy plants mentioned already and a lot more besides can be grown from seed. Apart from the savings, there is a great deal of pleasure to be gained from growing your own plants. For a beginner it can be a way of filling a border or even a garden fairly cheaply, and it does not matter half as much if a few plants die in winter.

Delphiniums can be raised readily from seed and this applies to most of the delphinium species too. For a little money enough good plants can be raised to satisfy all but the gardener with two acres of land to cultivate. The beauty of raising seedlings is that you never quite know what you are likely to obtain; remember how 'Daily Express', one of the most famous of delphiniums, was raised by Ronald Parrett from a packet of seed he purchased from Baker's. Plenty of other perennial plants are easy to propagate from seed, too, including aquilegias which can be used most effec-

Useful hardy plants which can be grown from seed
Achillea
Alchemilla mollis
Astrantia
Alstroemeria
Anthemis
Aquilegia
Astilbe
Campanula
Chrysanthemum maximum
Echinacea purpurea
Echinops ritro
Erigeron
Eryngium
Filipendula
Geranium
Geum
Gypsophila
Helenium
Hemerocallis
Incarvillea delavayi
Kniphofia
Liatris
Lupin
Lychnis chalcedonica
Lythrum
Monarda didyma
Penstemon
Phlox
Sedum
Sidalcea
Verbascum

This list is not exhaustive; there are a surprising number of plants which can be grown easily from seed

pink and red through to purple. Some people find alstroemeria seed difficult to germinate, while others seem to throw it down on the ground in autumn and the plant just comes up.

Some very comprehensive seed catalogues list many kinds of hardy plant seeds: echinops, lythrum, lychnis, penstemon and sidalcea, to pick just a few at random. I see that there is even a new strain of *Phlox paniculata* hybrids. Incidentally, phlox seed is best sown in trays in autumn and left to over winter. Germination will take place the following early spring and with fresh seed it will be surprisingly good.

THE WHITE BORDER

There is nothing new about white borders but for all that they are most attractive and can always be guaranteed to impress friends and neighbours. One particular merit is that they seem so tasteful and pleasingly restful.

Lovers of delphiniums have a head start if they decide to create such a border because white delphiniums make a grand display. Cultivars available are 'Demavand', lavender white, white eye; 'Icecap', pure white, white eye; 'Iona', white, black eye; 'Lilian Bassett', white, black eye; 'Moonbeam', pure white; 'Olive Poppleton', off-white, honey eye; 'Panda', white, black eye; 'Sandpiper', white, black eye; 'Snowdon', pale grey, brown eye. Planted in groups they look magnificent. Add a few pillar roses such as 'Sander's White', 'White Cockade' and 'Climbing Iceberg' and let the everlasting sweet pea, *Lathyrus latifolius*

tively in front of delphiniums as they move towards flowering. *Monarda* 'Panorama' is a seed strain readily available, the seeds germinate easily and the plants have a wide range of colour from

'White Pearl', climb through them and you will have a combination *par excellence*. The choice for the rest of the border is wide: *Campanula latifolia* 'Alba', *Campanula persicifolia* 'Planiflora Alba', *Chrysanthemum maximum*, dahlias, *Malva moschata* 'Alba', *Phlox* 'White Admiral', and *Physostegia* 'Summer Snow' are a few of the plants growers have used successfully in their white borders but there are plenty more to discover. In fact the search for plants to include in the border is one of the ultimate pleasures to be gained.

An additional charm is to include grey foliage plants, a somewhat neglected area of interest. Again, there is a fascination in discovering grey plants that will fit into the overall colour scheme. A few suggestions are *Artemisia absinthium* 'Lambrook Silver' (common wormwood), a hardy shrubby plant growing about 90 cm (3 ft) high which is readily obtained. The white sage, *Artemisia ludoviciana*, is an herbaceous perennial which grows between 60-120 cm (2-4 ft) tall. *Ballota pseudodictamnus* (horehound) is slightly tender

and can be caught by a frost, so until you are sure it will survive in your garden, cuttings should be taken. It is a good plant and, despite its name, is quite easily obtained. *Helichrysum augustifolium* (curry plant) is a short perennial with downy foliage; as its name implies, it smells of curry, but don't be put off by that. *Helichrysum petiolatum* has become very popular and 'Variegata' with its green and white foliage could fit into the scheme of things quite nicely. Taking stem cuttings is easy and it does not take long to build up a good number which can be useful for filling blank spaces at the front. Best treated as a half-hardy annual, *Senecio cineraria* 'Silver Dust' is an excellent low growing 'filler' too. A further suggestion is *Tanacetum haradjanii*, 15-20 cm (6–8 in) which is suitable for edging. It is hardy in well drained soil but needs full sun.

The permutations for a border of this kind are huge and can be tremendously rewarding. The only reservation must be on the size of such a border, because it needs to be large enough to look effective.

Delphiniums for a white border
'Demavand'
'Lilian Bassett'
'Moonbeam'
'Olive Poppleton'
'Panda'
'Royal Wedding'
'Sandpiper'
'Silver Jubilee'
'Snowdon'

THE SILVER AND PINK BORDER

I must admit that I have never seen such a border and so this is only an idea but with so many fine pink delphiniums available, it does strike me that a pink and silver/grey border could look fantastic. I listed above many grey and silver foliaged plants and there are a large number of pink-flowered hardy plants

Delphiniums for a pink and silver border
'Antares'
'Claire'
'Clifford Lass'
'Clifford Pink'
'Garden Party'
'Langdon's Royal Flush'
'Magic Moment'
'Our Deb'
'Pink Ruffles'
'Rosemary Brock'
'Ruby'
'Strawberry Fair'
'Summer Wine'
'Turkish Delight'

easily obtained – monarda, sidalcea, phlox and sedum to mention just a few. Equally, the number of pink delphiniums available is large, including the old favourites 'Turkish Delight', a pale pinkish mauve, white eye and completely perennial with me; 'Strawberry Fair', rich mulberry rose; 'Royal Flush', deep dusky pink, white eye; and 'Garden Party', pink, white eye. Amongst the newer cultivars are 'Claire', pale pink with a creamy pink eye; 'Clifford Pink', deep pink, creamy white eye; and 'Rosemary Brock', a wonderful deep dusky pink with a brown eye. All these produce really good spikes and I find them as perennial as any of my other delphiniums.

ISLAND BED

Mixed borders are fine and I have said a lot about them but there is a good case to be argued for island beds and, clearly, there is no rule that says you cannot have both. Island beds were pioneered by Alan Bloom as a good way of displaying hardy perennials to their best advantage. The tallest plants are placed in the centre and the shortest around the edge. Delphiniums look good in island beds with the only reservation being that because they need attention they must remain accessible. As far as the modern garden is concerned, island beds can be ideal for they can be quite small. Many of the modern delphiniums are reasonably short and cultivars like 'Blue Tit' and 'Cupid', which only grow to 90 cm (3 ft) or so, will fit into the tiniest bed.

GROWING DELPHINIUMS IN CONTAINERS

Many would-be delphinium lovers are totally restricted for space and yet would love to grow them, but there is nothing stopping them growing delphiniums in containers. In fact all the delphiniums on show at the Chelsea Flower Show are grown in pots. It would be stupid to pretend that the plant isn't happier in the open ground but for all that it is not difficult to get good results. It is probably best to start with a shorter cultivar such as 'Lord Butler', a bright blue with a white eye, or 'Loch Leven', a mid-blue, white eye. Order the plants early or take early cuttings so that they can be potted in late spring or early summer. The minimum pot size should be 13 cm (5 in), using a loam-based compost suitable for large plants. Although the plants need plenty of water, good drainage is important so crock the pot. As the plant grows it will need potting on to a larger pot. The final pot should not be less than 20cm (8in) although 25 or 30cm (10 or 12in) might be better depending on the size of the plant. The compost must be kept moist and the plants must not be allowed to dry out at any time. A regular weekly feed with a liquid fertilizer is necessary too. They will die down in winter but can stay outside. Although they do not need as much water and certainly do not require feeding, make sure the pots do not become totally dry. Slugs should be deterred with slug pellets at all times, including winter. When the new growth appears recommence the watering and gradually resume feeding. The shoots should be thinned to a maximum of three or four and must be staked with a short cane when they are 30cm (12in) high. Try not to keep the plants in too much shade and with luck a gorgeous display will be forthcoming.

DELPHINIUMS FOR ARRANGEMENTS

When one thinks of flowers for floral arrangements delphiniums are not usually the first to come to mind. This is rather sad because they can be used to make magnificent displays. In the Netherlands thousands of delphinium spikes are sold solely for flower arranging, but they are treated to stop them dropping their petals so quickly. My wife frequently uses delphiniums for altar arrangements in our church and they never fail to attract attention and much comment.

The snag is that large delphinium spikes which look wonderful in a church, would probably not fit too well in most family-size homes. One way around this is to use laterals which are smaller and are the ideal size and length for flower arrangements.

An even better answer is to grow a patch of Connecticut Yankee hybrids or a row of belladonna delphiniums. Both of these delphinium hybrids usually come into bloom in early summer, bearing dainty flowers on whippy stems. The Connecticut Yankee need to be raised from seed and are perennials but with a short life. Belladonna delphiniums can only be obtained as plants but they are very hardy and perennial. Flower arrangers will enjoy having them in the garden.

CHAPTER THREE

CHOOSING THE BEST: ELATUM CULTIVARS

The following selection is my choice of some of the best delphiniums available from specialist nurserymen. Each plant is judged on its overall merits and its worth in the garden and not merely as an exhibition plant. You may disagree with some of my more subjective remarks. That is the way it is in gardening and thank goodness for that, because it would be awful if we all liked the same thing. In fact the only way to know whether a plant is to your taste, is to see it. The only way to know whether a plant will flourish in your garden, is to grow it.

DESCRIPTIVE LIST OF NAMED ELATUM CULTIVARS

Readers should note that the heights quoted are an average to be expected when the plants are grown under normal conditions. The seasons are also only a guide and in a typical season 'early' would be roughly the middle of early summer, 'mid' the end of early summer and 'late' early mid-summer. The awards are those given by the Royal Horticultural Society following the trials at Wisley Garden: FCC – First Class Certificate, AM – Award of Merit and HC – Highly Commended.

'Alice Artindale'
This is an old, but unique cultivar which is loved by flower arrangers and by gardeners looking for something different to grow in their hardy plant borders. It is difficult to do justice in words to its appearance but its colour is rosy mauve edged with blue and it is fully double. The spike is thin and the florets small. It was raised in the 1930s, so it is getting rather ancient and plants available can be very variable.
Height: 1.5 m (5 ft)   Season: Early
Raiser: W. Artindale
Year of Introduction: 1935   Award: FCC 1951

'Baby Doll'
During the 1960s there were a number of 'dwarf' delphiniums introduced. It was thought that by being shorter these would require less staking and be more suitable for the small garden.

Unfortunately, today's breeders have forgotten about this and do not raise many, if any, shorter cultivars. 'Baby Doll' is too old to be a baby and not very dwarf either because it can be quite tall at 1.5 m (5 ft) in certain seasons and conditions. Nonetheless it is still a charming pale mauve plant with a white eye.
Height: 1.2 m (4 ft).   Season: Mid
Raiser: Blackmore & Langdon
Year or Introduction: 1964   Award: AM 1977

'Blue Nile'
This plant has been around for a long time but for sheer colour it still takes a lot of beating. It is usually described as brilliant mid-blue with a white eye but this does not convey the full impact it can have in the right setting. It appears to grow better in some gardens than others but it is always worth a trial.
Height: 1.65 m (5½ ft)   Season: Mid
Raiser: Blackmore & Langdon
Year of Introduction: 1962   Award: FCC 1966

'Blue Tit'
'Blue Tit' was the first of the 'dwarf' delphiniums and is still growing well. Some so-called 'dwarf' plants can reach 1.5 m (5 ft) but 'Blue Tit' always remains short. The colour, indigo blue with a white eye, is not that inspiring but its value lies in its height and constitution.
Height: 1.05 m (3½ ft)   Season: Early
Raiser: Blackmore & Langdon
Year of Introduction: 1956   Award: FCC 1961

Although an old favourite, 'Blue Nile' is still unsurpassed for its brilliance and colour.

(Opposite) *Often a winner on the show bench, 'Bruce' also makes a fine garden plant.*

(Above) *One of the later flowering delphiniums, 'Conspicuous' lives up to its name.*

'Bruce'
Violet purple with a dark brown eye, this cultivar is usually thought of as an exhibition plant but with reasonable attention it can look well in the border, for example providing a lovely background to bright yellow hemerocallis (day lilies). It is perennial and throws a good number of shoots. However, it does need to be supported early or the spikes will fall down.
Height: 1.8 m (6 ft)   Season: Mid
Raiser: D. McGlashan
Year of Introduction: 1977   Awards: FCC 1986

'Butterball'
Light cream with a yellow eye, 'Butterball' perhaps provides as good a chance as any for the gardener to grow a cream delphinium. It does grow better on some soils than others but is usually quite reliable. The spikes are short and stumpy and to get them to a reasonable height feeding needs to be generous.
Height: 1.35 m (4½ ft)   Season: Mid
Raiser: Blackmore & Langdon
Year of Introduction: 1966   Award: FCC 1988

'Can Can'
This newcomer is not to everyone's taste but those who like 'Alice Artindale' may well approve of 'Can Can'. It is double with pinky mauve/blue florets, layered to give a frilly effect.
Height: 1.35 m (4½ ft)   Season: Mid
Raiser: D. McGlashan
Year of Introduction: 1986   Award: HC 1987

'Cassius'
A sturdy plant for a dark contrast, this purple with a white eye is reliable and perennial and fills a gap in the delphinium colour range.
Height: 1.65 m (5½ ft)   Season: Mid
Raiser: Blackmore & Langdon
Year of Introduction: 1976   Award: HC 1979

'Chelsea Star'
The feature of this plant is its colour, a beautiful velvety-violet purple with a contrasting white eye. Unfortunately, it can be prone to mildew and its perenniality is suspect so plenty of cuttings should be taken. To complete the list of faults, it is also rather gappy. However, until a better plant comes along it is worth persevering with and it can be used with great effect in the garden.
Height: 1.65 m (5½ ft)   Season: Mid
Raiser: Blackmore & Langdon
Year of Introduction: 1975   Award: FCC 1986

'Claire'
This is a new introduction from Colin Edwards (a well known amateur raiser and delphinium writer) which is a short pale pink with a pinkish white eye. Apparently, its strong feature is its ability to hold its bottom florets so that the complete spike can be in flower at the same time. It is certainly an attractive looking plant and will look well in the garden.
Height: 1.5 m (5 ft)   Season: Mid
Raiser: C. R. Edwards
Year of Introduction: 1984

'Clifford Pink'
The florets of 'Clifford Pink' are very pretty, neat and deep pink with a creamy white eye. The darkish stems help to emphasize the colour, and overall the plant has a well proportioned look about it. A nice group of these would brighten a border and contrast well with darker plants.
Height: 1.65 m (5½ ft)   Season: Mid
Raiser: Woodfield Bros
Year of Introduction: 1984   Award: HC 1986

'Conspicuous'
As with most things there are fads with delphiniums and at one time there were quite a few delphinium cultivars with dark contrasting eyes. Now there are very few. 'Conspicuous' has rounded florets of light mauve with a brown eye and it shows up well, but is not very perennial so that cuttings should be taken regularly.
Height: 1.5 m (5 ft)   Season: Late
Raiser: Blackmore & Langdon
Year of Introduction: 1963   Award: FCC 1970

'Crown Jewel'
'Crown Jewel' has a large prominent black eye which contrasts with the mid-blue petals of the floret. Its spikes are not of exhibition quality but it is a good garden plant and throws up a lot of shoots.
Height: 1.5 m (5 ft)   Season: Mid
Raiser: Blackmore & Langdon
Year of Introduction: 1977   Award: AM 1979

'Cupid'
A very nice little plant for a small border and another genuine short. 'Cupid' has pale sky blue florets with a white eye.
Height: 1.05 m (3 ft)   Season: Mid
Raiser: Blackmore & Langdon
Year of Introduction: 1964   Award: AM 1969

'Demavand'
If I have a favourite 'white' delphinium this is probably the one. It was raised by Ronald Parrett and has white petals with pale lavender on the back giving the florets an off-white look; the eye is white. With me it does not grow very tall, mostly because it is not thinned drastically, and so year after year I get a grand display of shortish white columns.
Height: 1.35 m (4½ ft)   Season: Early
Raiser: R. Parrett
Year of Introduction: 1970   Award: HC 1980

'Dolly Bird'
'Dolly Bird' is not a delphinium perfectionist's delight. The colour is good, a very pale mauve with a white eye, but the florets are often rather spaced giving a gappy look. This will not worry the gardener looking for cool shades for the garden and the plant has a lot going for it in the way of reliability.
Height: 1.5 m (5 ft)   Season: Mid
Raiser: Blackmore & Langdon
Year of Introduction: 1979

'Emily Hawkins'
One of the neatest looking of all delphiniums, 'Emily Hawkins' has light lavender blue florets with a light beige

(Opposite) *A first class perennial plant, 'Emily Hawkins' gives a good account of itself most years.*

(Above) *The perennial 'Fanfare' has been around for 30 years but still has plenty of vigour.*

and lavender eye carried on whippy stems. A good perennial which will give a good show early each season.
Height: 1.65 m (5½ ft) Season: Early
Raiser: D. W. Bassett
Year of Introduction: 1980 Award: FCC 1983

'Fanfare'
Another cultivar guaranteed to give early season flowers, this old favourite has been around for years but still has plenty of vigour left in her. The flat florets are silvery mauve with a white eye. Completely perennial it can be used with great effect as an early summer backdrop.
Height: 1.8 m (6 ft) Season: Early
Raiser: Blackmore & Langdon
Year of Introduction: 1960 Award: FCC 1964

'Faust'
If a tall reliable dark blue delphinium is required for the garden, this is the one. Its colour is usually described as ultramarine blue with an indigo/blue eye and the spike is rather slender giving the overall habit a fastigiate effect.
Height: 1.8 m (6 ft) Season: Mid
Raiser: Blackmore & Langdon
Year of Introduction: 1965 Award: FCC 1975

'Fenella'
Yet another plant which should be grown for its colour, 'Fenella' has pure gentian blue florets with a black eye flecked with purple, making it almost radiant in appearance.
Height: 1.5 m (5 ft) Season: Mid
Raiser: Blackmore & Langdon

Year of Introduction: 1964 Award: AM 1968

'Gillian Dallas'
This is a delightful garden plant with large pale lavender florets and a white eye with violet markings. The spikes have a tidy and tapered look about them although they need to be well supported because the stems break in windy weather.
Height: 1.5 m (5 ft) Season: Mid
Raiser: Blackmore & Langdon
Year of Introduction: 1972 Award: FCC 1984

'Giotto'
A new plant which is very pleasing in appearance, having slightly frilled florets with inner petals which are mauve and outer ones of blue, all complemented by a light brown eye.
Height: 1.8 m (6 ft) Season: Mid
Raiser: D. W. Bassett
Year of Introduction: 1986 Award: AM 1988

'Gordon Forsyth'
This is a fine delphinium that has tall and tapered spikes which fit beautifully into a garden display. The pale amethyst florets with a small dark eye have a lighter centre and frilled edges giving almost a hollyhock look to the flowers but not to the overall look of the plant.
Height: 1.8 m (6 ft) Season: Mid
Raiser: Blackmore & Langdon
Year of Introduction: 1969 Award: FCC 1986

'Gossamer'
The amateur raiser, the late Tom

Cowan, longed to breed a turquoise delphinium; he never succeeded but he got a very greenish look to some of his plants. 'Gossamer' is pale mauve-blue with a distinctive green tinge. Admittedly this green can vary depending on the soil but it can be very attractive. Given the right companions, a small group of 'Gossamer' with this greenish look can be used most effectively to produce a lush effect.
Height: 1.5 m (5 ft)　Season: Mid
Raiser: T. O. Cowan
Year of Introduction: 1972　Award: AM 1984

'Guy Langdon'

This cultivar is the odd man out because it was the premier exhibition plant of its time and is nearly always grown for that purpose. As a plant it leaves a bit to be desired because it does not usually live that long; indeed the raisers did not keep it in their catalogue for any length of time for that reason. It can produce enormous spikes and might be considered a bit gross but the satisfaction when a good spike is grown is tremendous. It is probably past its best because it is not seen on the show benches so much now, but it's still well worth growing. The colour is royal purple with a purple and white striped eye.
Height: 1.8 m (6 ft)　Season: Mid
Raiser: Blackmore & Langdon
Year of Introduction: 1957　Award: FCC 1958

'Hilda Lucas'

Extending the delphinium flowering season is a must in the border and this cultivar can be a great help, for it is the latest of all delphiniums to flower. On top of which, it is a grand plant of perfect shape and form, fully perennial and with good flowers. The floret colour is pinkish mauve tinged with blue and, while it is, not perhaps the easiest plant from which to root cuttings, it is well worth obtaining.
Height: 1.65 m (5½ ft)　Season: Late
Raiser: H. R. Lucas
Year of Introduction: 1961　Award: FCC 1978

'Kathleen Cooke'

The 'experts' always maintained that any seedlings from 'Blue Nile' would be poor, until Jim Cooke proved them wrong by producing 'Kathleen Cooke', a cross between 'Loch Nevis' and 'Blue Nile'. This cultivar is a very nice mid-blue with a white eye and spikes which are long and tapering. It is a good doer although for the purist the florets are too close together. For those looking for a bright blue garden display 'Kathleen Cooke' could be a nice addition to their collection.
Height: 1.65 m (5½ ft)　Season: Mid
Raiser: J. A. Cooke
Year of Introduction: 1984　Award: AM 1987

'Langdon's Royal Flush'

This cultivar can produce really good symmetrical spikes in a nice shade of deep pink with a white eye. However, it can be inconsistent and sometimes miss out the following season by having inferior spikes. But worth a place in the garden for the good years.

The dark blue 'Fenella' makes a fine display, especially when grown with delphiniums of contrasting colour.

The florets of 'Gillian Dallas' have a perfect shape which gives a tidy look to the plant.

Height: 1.35 m (4½ ft)   Season: Mid
Raiser: Blackmore & Langdon
Year of Introduction: 1975   Award:
AM 1986

'Layla'
This list includes some very old plants
but 'Layla' is brand new. Predicting the
future for delphiniums is chancy but this
pale cream with a yellow-brown eye
would appear to have a good one in
front of it. 'Layla' has a pretty, slightly
frilled floret giving a graceful feminine
appearance; it should look extremely
nice when associated with other quietly
coloured plants, for example the shrub
rose 'Penelope'.
Height: 1.65 m (5½ ft)   Season: Mid
Raiser: C. D. Moffatt
Year of Introduction: 1987   Award: HC
1988

'Leonora'
Some plants attract all the attention
while others gradually find favour.
'Leonora' is a plant that has been
around awhile but often appears to get
overlooked. This is a pity because it is
quite a vigorous plant in a nice shade of
china blue with a prominent white eye.
All in all, it is a delphinium which shows
up well in the border, or rather would, if
it were grown more.
Height: 1.65 m (5½ ft)   Season: Mid
Raiser: R. Latty
Year of Introduction: 1969   Award:
AM 1984

'Lilian Bassett'
This is quite a new cultivar but appears
to be a perfect delphinium for garden
use. It is white with a prominent black

eye. As with most of David Bassett's
plants, its form is good and its general
appearance neat. It is fairly short and
one suspects that the ideal way to use it
in the border is not to over thin but to
allow it to produce a fair number of its
slim and whippy spikes.
Height: 1.5 m (5 ft)   Season: Mid
Raiser: D. W. Bassett
Year of Introduction: 1984   Award:
AM 1988

'Loch Leven'
This plant is nearly the ideal garden
delphinium: ideal height, good shape
and form, beautiful colour (soft mid-
blue with a white eye) and quite
reliable. In fact all delphinium lovers
should grow 'Loch Leven'. And the
criticisms? The eye could be neater and
the colour has a trace of pink in it which
slightly spoils the blue. Finally, the plant
is quite old now so it is important that
any new plants should come from good
stock.
Height: 1.65 m (5½ ft)   Season: Mid
Raiser: T. O. Cowan
Year of Introduction: 1969   Award:
FCC 1974

'Loch Nevis'
'Loch Nevis' was raised from a seed
which came from the same pod as the
one which produced 'Loch Leven'. As
with 'Guy Langdon', mentioned earlier,
'Loch Nevis' once won scores of prizes
but nowadays is seen far less often on
the show benches. It is similar in many
respects to 'Loch Leven', mid-blue and
a white eye, but is taller. Accordingly, it
looks extremely good in the border.
Unfortunately, the years have taken

their toll and it does appear to have deteriorated, but if a good plant were to come to hand it should be grown.
Height: 1.8 m (6 ft) Season: Mid
Raiser: T. O. Cowan
Year of Introduction: 1969 Award: FCC 1970

'Lord Butler'
This is an excellent little plant, another of those delphiniums ideally suited to the small garden. The colour is pale Cambridge blue with a white eye and the habit is semi-dwarf. It is vigorous and throws up a number of spikes, so that to over thin might be to lose its best effect, as a multi-stemmed but short plant.
Height: 1.35 m (4½ ft) Season: Mid
Raiser: Blackmore & Langdon
Year of Introduction: 1968 Award: AM 1970

'Michael Ayres'
This solid looking plant has rich violet florets with a black eye, a perfect foil for other lighter coloured plants.
Height: 1.8 m (6 ft) Season: Mid
Raiser: Blackmore & Langdon
Year of Introduction: 1962 Award: AM 1975

'Mighty Atom'
'Mighty Atom' lives up to its name for it is a shortish but vigorous plant with large florets. To be honest its colour of deep lavender is not very exciting but it is a clear colour which in the right setting would contrast ideally with a glistening white flower such as *Lavatera trimestris* 'Mont Blanc'. The snag with 'Mighty Atom' is that it is prone to both fasciation and mildew, but it is still a plant to grow.
Height: 1.35 m (4½ ft) Season: Late
Raiser: Blackmore & Langdon
Year of Introduction: 1968 Award: FCC 1975

'Min'
Another very new plant raised by Duncan McGlashan who introduced 'Bruce'. 'Min' is a robust plant with pale lavender florets veined with deep lavender and a brown and lavender eye. The spikes are large and tapering and clearly suitable for showing but the colouring is such that its possibilities must also lie in the border.
Height: 1.65 m (5½ ft) Season: Mid
Raiser: D. McGlashan
Year of Introduction: 1986 Award: HC 1988

'Molly Buchanan'
The two qualities which still make 'Molly Buchanan' a possibility for the garden are its colour and its late flowering. The florets are an intense gentian blue with a black eye and although spike length and floret size could be better there is no other cultivar quite that shade.
Height: 1.65 m (5½ ft) Season: Late
Raiser: Blackmore & Langdon
Year of Introduction: 1960 Award: HC 1962

'Moonbeam'
Pure white delphinium cultivars are noticeable by their absence. No doubt breeders are busy trying to fill the gap but meanwhile 'Moonbeam' has to be the choice. However, it could be better

'Giotto', a new delphinium raised by David Bassett, which received an Award of Merit in 1988.

Introduced in 1969 'Gordon Forsyth' remains one of the finest delphiniums in cultivation.

in form as it has a thin spike and the
florets are uneven.
Height: 1.65 m (5½ ft)   Season: Mid
Raiser: Blackmore & Langdon
Year of Introduction: 1963

'Nimrod'
'Nimrod' is a Mr. Reliable of the
delphinium world, and gives a display
whatever the season, with its sturdy
stems carrying smallish flowers. It has
bright purple florets, slightly lighter in
the centre, outside petals tinged with
royal blue, while the eye is white with
some purple in it. Perhaps not the most
elegant of cultivars and it can be very
tall, but it's most useful.
Height: 2 m (6½ ft)   Season: Mid
Raiser: Blackmore & Langdon
Year of Introduction: 1973   Award:
AM 1975

'Olive Poppleton'
This is a truly beautiful plant, large
white florets with a contrasting golden-
honey eye, carried in graceful spikes. It
does drop its bottom florets a little too
soon but it still gives a grand display. It
can also lack perenniality in heavy soils,
so cuttings should be taken.
Height: 1.65 m (5½ ft)   Season: Mid
Raiser: R. J. E. Poppleton
Year of Introduction: 1972   Award:
FCC 1980

'Pericles'
'Pericles' is a nice delphinium, having
soft mid-blue florets with a white eye. It
grows well and easily, and its clear blue
colouring shows up well, making it an
effective plant to have in the mixed
border.

Height: 1.65 m (5½ ft)   Season: Mid
Raiser: Blackmore & Langdon
Year of Introduction: 1975

'Pink Ruffles'
A somewhat unusual cultivar, 'Pink
Ruffles', as its name implies, has double
florets of very pale pink. These grow on
a stocky spike making it not the most
graceful of delphiniums but worth
considering by those who like double
cultivars.
Height: 1.5 m (5 ft)   Season: Mid
Raiser: Blackmore & Langdon
Year of Introduction: 1985

'Rosemary Brock'
'Rosemary Brock' is arguably the best
of the 'pinks'. The neat florets are dusky
pink with edges of a deeper shade, the
eye is deep brown touched with rose and
has heavy yellow hairs. The effect is eye
catching. The form is good with slim
whippy stems and good foliage. As with
most pinks a slightly shaded site is
preferable if the full colour effect is to
be seen, as too much sun will soon
bleach flowers.
Height: 1.5 m (5 ft)   Season: Mid
Raiser: D. W. Bassett
Year of Introduction: 1984   Award:
AM 1985

'Sabrina'
Another useful short plant, a bright
pure blue with a white eye which flowers
early and has a good constitution.
Height: 1.2 m (4 ft)   Season: Early
Raiser: Blackmore & Langdon
Year of Introduction: 1962

'Sandpiper'
This delphinium flowers early and immediately catches the attention because of its large white florets and prominent black eye. It is attractive and easy to grow.
Height: 1.65 m (5½ft) Season: Early
Raiser: R. Latty
Year of Introduction: 1977 Award: FCC 1980

'Savrola'
Another plant which has never had a lot of attention in delphinium circles and yet after thirty years it is still being grown. It is still vigorous and the colour is attractive, being a rich blue and plum purple with a brown eye. The petals are slightly frilled which adds to the appeal. Still a good border plant.
Height: 1.8 m (6 ft) Season: Mid
Raiser: Blackmore & Langdon
Year of Introduction: 1959 Award: AM 1964

'Sentinel'
'Sentinel' well and truly stands guard over other plants in the garden. It can grow to over 2.1. m (7 ft) tall but stands up to attention well. Its colour is a bit stern, deep purple with a black and gold eye, but it adds dignity to the border.
Height: 2.1 m (7 ft) Season: Early
Raiser: Blackmore & Langdon
Year of Introduction: 1961 Award: FCC 1966

'Shimmer'
The bright blue of 'Blue Nile' is exquisite but that cultivar can be unreliable in some gardens. 'Shimmer' is an alternative. It is nearly as bright, having mid-blue florets and a white eye, but is taller and in some gardens far more reliable. Another advantage worth considering is that it flowers later in the season.
Height: 1.8 m (6 ft) Season: Late
Raiser: Blackmore & Langdon
Year of Introduction: 1970 Award: AM 1975

'Silver Jubilee'
This is another white with a dark eye, quite a strong growing plant and one to consider if white delphiniums appeal or if a white border is being considered.
Height: 1.65 m (5½ft) Season: Mid
Raiser: Blackmore & Langdon
Year of Introduction: 1977 Award: HC 1981

'Silver Moon'
In its day 'Silver Moon' was one of the all time greats, a breakthrough not in colour but in form. A pyramidal spike, large florets and petals with great texture. The colour is silver-mauve with a white eye. The years have caught up and it is not as outstanding as it was but it still looks good and is a reliable plant to have in the garden.
Height: 1.8 m (6 ft) Season: Mid
Raiser: Blackmore & Langdon
Year of Introduction: 1953 Award: FCC 1956

'Skyline'
For those who love blue delphiniums 'Skyline' must score high. It is a flower, as its name suggests, as blue as a clear summer's sky and because the large eye is blue too, it has an almost double look. The overall look of the plant is good and

(Above) *'Leonora' has never been widely grown but it's a very worthwhile delphinium to consider.*

(Opposite) *Raised by the late Tom Cowan, 'Loch Leven' is an ideal garden delphinium, beautiful in colour and quite reliable.*

it can look truly excellent in the right setting. Another late-flowering plant to extend the flowering period.
Height: 1.5 m (5 ft)   Season: Late
Raiser: Blackmore & Langdon
Year of Introduction: 1970   Award: AM 1976

'Snowdon'
'Snowdon' is a plant with a difference. The florets are an off-white while the eye is a light honey colour. It is, however, the stems of the spikes which distinguish it because they are a dark, almost bronze colour. These are tall and, because the length of spike is not large, the dark stems appear beneath the skirt of white flowers and, also, peek through any gaps in the florets, giving a distinctive and attractive look to the plant. The stems are fairly weak and the plant needs staking as soon as possible.
Height: 1.8 m (6 ft)   Season: Mid
Raiser: R. Latty
Year of Introduction: 1971   Award: FCC 1983

'Spindrift'
The colour of some delphiniums varies tremendously from season to season and from soil to soil; such a one is 'Spindrift' which is usually described, very baldly, as greenish blue and turquoise. The colour combination is impossible to set down accurately, especially as it can change according to circumstance: sometimes it is mostly blue with no apparent green, at other times it has a distinct greenish cast. It is a fascinating plant to grow and flower arrangers love it; it also has a good spike and has won

prizes in shows. Easy to propagate, it clearly has many applications in the garden.
Height: 1.65 m (5½ ft)   Season: Early
Raiser: T. O. Cowan
Year of Introduction: 1971   Award: AM 1973

'Strawberry Fair'
With many new pinks being raised 'Strawberry Fair', which has been available since 1968, has much competition. However, it still does have one or two merits which make it a plant useful to have. The colour is mulberry rose with a white eye and both the florets and the eye are neat and tidy. The form of the spike is quite good and the stems are strong so that it does not succumb easily during storms. Generally, it is a very reliable grower and will look good in most seasons.
Height: 1.5 m (5 ft)   Season: Mid
Raiser: Blackmore & Langdon
Year of Introduction: 1968   Award: FCC 1983

'Sungleam'
'Sungleam' is a creamy-yellow cultivar with a canary-yellow eye and some people find it easier to grow than 'Butterball'. When growing well it is extremely attractive and complements the blue delphiniums beautifully. It needs good cultivation to see it at its best.
Height: 1.5 m (5 ft)   Season: Mid
Raiser: Blackmore & Langdon
Year of Introduction: 1971   Award: FCC 1984

'Thundercloud'

This cultivar can look a little dull because its colour is deep purple with a black eye but it's another of those tall cultivars which can be a first class background to more colourful plants.
Height: 1.8 m (6 ft)   Season: Mid
Raiser: Blackmore & Langdon
Year of Introduction: 1971   Award: AM 1975

'Tiddles'

This delphinium has a double look which some people like and others hate. The florets are slate mauve in colour and a bit untidy in appearance. The spikes are a little short and sturdy but the overall effect is not displeasing.
Height: 1.5 m (5 ft)   Season: Mid
Raiser: Blackmore & Langdon
Year of Introduction: 1963   Award: FCC 1971

'Tiny Tim'

Although this is an allegedly short delphinium its main appeal lies with its colour: deep blue flushed mauve, which gives it a certain luminosity. A small group of 'Tiny Tim' can make a bright little feature in a small design but it can make a larger one too because its height can vary.
Height: 1.0–1.5 m (3½–5 ft)   Season: Mid
Raiser: Blackmore & Langdon
Year of Introduction: 1972   Award: AM 1979

'Turkish Delight'

'Turkish Delight' is actually light mauve but with its white eye it looks pale pink. A very reliable plant, its spike is neat and tapering. It is still a very useful plant, providing a cool and subdued contrast in the border.
Height: 1.65 m (5½ ft)   Season: Mid
Raiser: Blackmore & Langdon
Year of Introduction: 1966   Award: FCC 1979

'Vespers'

The spikes produced by 'Vespers' are tapering and well shaped. This combined with blue and mauve florets and a white eye make this an attractive border delphinium.
Height: 1.65 m (5½ ft)   Season: Mid
Raiser: Blackmore & Langdon
Year of Introduction: 1962   Award: AM 1979

CHAPTER FOUR

CHOOSING THE BEST:
THE SPECIES AND THEIR HYBRIDS

There are well over 300 delphinium
species growing wild throughout the
world – the exact number depends on
which botanical authority is taken.
These species can be perennial, annual
and sometimes biennial. Many grow in
high and sometimes mountainous conditions and most look quite unlike our
border delphinium. They can be fascinating to grow and sometimes surprisingly easy. For the person who likes
growing plants from seed and seeing
what arises, they provide much pleasure. Here are just a few to try:

Consolida ambigua (Delphinium ajacis)
(rocket larkspur)
Originating from the Swiss Alps this annual is thought to be one of the parents of the modern larkspur, the other candidate being *Consolida regalis*. Growing about 30–90 cm (1–3 ft) tall with a spread of 30 cm (12 in), the blue or violet flowers are borne in loose racemes, up to 60 cm (24 in) long, on erect slightly branched stems during early-mid summer. It is easy to grow from seed sown in early spring.

Consolida regalis (Delphinium consolida)
(field larkspur)
This is an annual delphinium from Northern Europe. It is quite attractive and grows between 45–75 cm (18–30 in) high with a spread of 30–38 cm (12–15 in) in a rather mound like habit. The small open flowers which are produced on many branching and erect stems are violet blue in colour and have uptilted spurs, while the foliage is finely cut and mid-green. An excellent cut flower and useful in the border with the clouds of bloom making a nice effect. It is very easy to raise from seed and a sowing in early spring will give flowers by mid-summer which last for a number of weeks. Plenty of seed is produced and the plant often produces self sown off-spring the following year.

D. cardinale
This plant still grows in profusion in some areas of California. Growing around 45–75 cm (1½–2½ ft) tall with a spread of about 30 cm (12 in), it produces loose racemes of cup-shaped florets 23–30 cm (9–12 in) long on wirey stems in mid to late summer. These florets are bright scarlet shaded yellow towards the centre. The foliage is palmate, deeply dissected and mid-green. Although it is hardy it is not very perennial in England and does not survive the damp winters so it needs to be grown from seed annually. Unfortunately, germination can sometimes be sporadic. Coming from sunny California it likes as warm and well-drained a site as can be found.

D. formosum
This is a graceful plant from the Swiss Alps which has violet blue florets and handsome grey-green palmate foliage. It grows about 60–90 cm (2–3 ft) tall and flowers from mid-summer onwards if grown as an annual. Easily raised from seed it can be sown in the open ground during late spring or early summer and transplanted in autumn for an early display. The first flowers will be over by mid-summer but if the stalks are promptly cut down instead of being allowed to seed, there will be a second display later in the year.

D. grandiflorum (syn *D. chinensis*)
This group from Russia and China embraces a large number of botanical varieties as well as several commercial strains. Growing about 30–38 cm (12–15 in) high with a spread of 23 cm (9 in), they are hardy perennials with deeply cut, palmately divided leaves. The deep violet-blue, open florets are borne individually on branching stems in mid-summer.

'Blue Butterfly' is a strain commonly grown, usually as a half-hardy annual which flowers for most of the summer from a sowing made in late winter or early spring. The plants are neat and compact and the flowers a beautiful rich blue. There are also light blue, lavender and white forms.

Another selection is *D. grandiflorum* 'Blue Mirror', a beautiful Cambridge blue dwarf introduced by M. Gaugin of Orleans in 1901. The large round florets have their brilliance enhanced by white eyes. Only 15–25 cm high it grows well in light sandy soil rich in humus.

D. nudicaule

This charming little plant comes from California and is a delightful flower for the small rock garden. It grows only about 30 cm (12 in) high, slightly taller in a good year, and it bears bright half-closed vermilion red flowers with red yellow throats in loose panicles on sturdy stems giving it a slightly bushy appearance. The flowers, which have a long spur, are produced between mid-spring and mid-summer depending on when the seed was sown. The leaves are somewhat fleshy and are divided into three notched leaflets.

It is a rather short-lived perennial and although hardy is best treated as an annual with new plants being raised each year. They are easy to raise from seed. The seed should be sown into pots filled with a good seed compost during early or late spring. Covered by a piece of cling film, the pots can be kept in a cold frame or similar until germination takes place, usually in three to four weeks. When the little plants are big enough to be handled they can be individually pricked out into pots. Later when they have made sufficient growth and when the weather is amenable they can be planted out into their flowering positions. They are pretty plants but to look anything there needs to be a few planted fairly close together, 15 cm (6 in) or so apart. It is quite possible to collect and harvest the seed for early sowing the following season.

D. nudicaule prefers a warm and well-drained position so a fairly sunny and open site is required, but provided the soil is not too cold and heavy it will flower readily with very little attention apart from taking the always necessary precautions against slugs. *D. nudicaule* makes quite a good pot plant for the greenhouse although it should be watched for the presence of red spider which seems to like delphinium species.

On a note of interest, during the 1930s Theodore Ruys of Royal Moerheim Nurseries, Holland, spent many years trying to obtain a red border delphinium by crossing *D. nudicaule* with *D. elatum* but had no luck until he spotted a natural mutation in a batch of *D. nudicaule* growing on his nursery. Persevering with crossing this with *D. elatum* a seedling was obtained; only a mere 12 cm (4½ in) high, it had dull purple flowers but fertile seed. He did not give in and the second generation produced the plant he was looking for: a plant rather like a belladonna delphinium but with straight stems and light rose flowers. It was named *D. ruysii* 'Pink Sensation' and introduced in 1936. It is still a nice border plant although not grown as widely as it was.

'Lord Butler' is a semi-dwarf plant which makes it suitable for the small garden.

D. tatsienense

This is a really worthwhile plant which comes from China. Growing about 30–45 cm (12–18 in) high, it produces long-spurred trumpet-shaped florets of brilliant cornflower blue with azure tips to the sepals and hooded eyes in the same colour. There is also a white form to grow as a companion. The florets are held in 15 cm (6 in) panicles on several branches and are produced in early to mid-summer. A vigorous species, some of the seedlings can grow into quite large clumps nearly 60 cm (2 ft) across but it is best planted fairly close at 15–23 cm (6–9 in) apart. However, a few twigs will support the foliage which consists of divided dark green leaves. *D. tatsienense* is a short-lived perennial suitable for rock gardens but new plants should be grown annually from seed. After flowering, seed is produced in abundance so that it can be harvested and used later.

D. zalil

This is an almost legendary flower which comes from Afghanistan and Iran. The flowers are pure sulphur yellow with orange tips to the two central sepals of each floret. The spikes extend to a height of 90–120 cm (3–4 ft) with a spread of 23 cm (9 in) above the delicate fern-like foliage. It has been grown in cultivation for many years and Kelways Nurseries gained an Award of Merit when it was exhibited at the Royal Horticultural Society's hall in 1891.

D. zalil germinates well but resents disturbance and therefore transplanting should be avoided as far as possible. A few seeds should be sown in small peat pots filled with seed compost in early spring and, without any further pricking out, they should be transplanted into a light well-drained open situation or perhaps into a larger pot. Great care should be taken not to damage the thong-like tap root and it is quite a good idea to remove the bottom of the pot at an early stage. Alternatively, it is possible to germinate the seed on damp kitchen roll and to place it carefully in a small peat pot as soon as the small root shows.

By autumn the plants will have developed tuberous roots and if they are in pots they can be kept in a frame to over winter. Those in the open ground can be dug up to avoid facing a winter in cold, damp soil and stored in a large pot of sandy soil. They need to be kept fairly dry and when there is any foliage an occasional dusting with malathion will deter red spider. And don't forget those slugs!

The following spring the plants should revive and can be planted out in that light, well-drained and open position, hopefully to produce good spikes in early summer.

> *Other species worth trying if obtainable*
>
> D. brunonianum
> D. cashmeriana
> D .leroyi
> D. welbeyi

OTHER DELPHINIUM HYBRIDS

There are a few garden hybrids which are different from the garden or elatum delphinium.

BELLADONNAS

The belladonna delphinium has been in cultivation for well over 100 years although its origins seem to be unknown. It has had its adherents and is well liked by many people but it can never be said to have been popular. It has not the grandeur and stateliness of the elatum delphinium but it has some merits.

The dainty florets are single, small and cup shaped, about 2 cm (¾ in) across, carried in loose spikes on slender but wiry stems. The foliage is small and deeply cut. Growing around 90–120 cm (3–4 ft) high with a fair number of the graceful branched spikes, the spread is 45–60 cm (18–24 in).

Belladonnas are not difficult to grow, their perenniality is good and their constitution strong. To grow at their best they should be planted in a sunny position with well-prepared soil. They can be grown singly but do look a little lost in a large border so that a group of three or more is probably to be preferred. Spacing should be approximately 60 cm (2 ft). They normally flower twice a year but if they are cut hard back can produce a third flush. They are a first class cut flower and often grown for flower arranging purposes.

Propagation of belladonna delphiniums is similar to elatum delphiniums, although shoots are more readily available, with cuttings taken in early spring.

Recommended cultivars are:

'Blue Bees'
A free-flowering plant that flowers early growing about 90 cm (3 ft) high. It has clear pale blue florets with a white eye. It was introduced in 1920.

'Capri'
This was a mutation occurring as one stem of the seedling which is now called 'Moorheimi'. It is light blue and usually flowers in early summer and again in mid-autumn. Both 'Capri' and 'Moorheimi' were raised at the Royal Moorheim Nurseries in Holland around 1900. Height 90 cm (3 ft).

'Lamartine'
Raised by the famous Victor Lemoine in 1903, it has a single flower of violet blue. It grows about 105 cm (3½ ft), flowering in early summer and mid-autumn.

'Moorheimi'
A single white which again flowers in early summer and mid-autumn. Again, its height is around 90 cm (3 ft).

'Naples'
Naples has semi-double, brilliant gentian blue flowers and was raised by Thompson and Morgan of Ipswich in 1930. Flowering around early summer, it grows 90 cm (3 ft) tall.

'Pink Sensation'
Not a true belladonna (see *D.*

nudicaule) it has yellowish pink buds which set off the dainty dullish pink flowers which hang a little on close spikes. It is a strong grower with a nice panopy of glossy leaves. Quite a good cut flower, it is a bit shorter, usually 75 cm–90 cm (2½–3 ft) and flowers in early summer and mid-autumn.

'Wendy'

Raised by Tommy Carlile, a founder of the Delphinium Society, in 1932 this has gentian blue flowers, the tips of the petals touched with purple, and a white eye. It flowers in early summer at around 90–105 cm (3–3½ ft) high.

THE CONNECTICUT YANKEES

This strain of seeds was originated by Edward Steichen and introduced in the early 1960s. They are hybrids resulting from a good deal of work on belladonna delphiniums, *D. elatum* and *D. tatsienense*. The flowers are single but have a small hooded eye usually of a creamy colour and sometimes edged with the colour of the petals. The colour range is purple, dark blue, light blue and white although the predominant colour is light blue and it is in this shade that larger individual florets are found. The plants are branching in habit reaching a height of only 90 cm (3 ft). They are good for flower arranging because the main stem and laterals come out at the same time. Seed is probably best sown under glass in early spring, with a little gentle heat. In this way flowers will be seen in the late summer and early autumn of the same year. Seed germination is good and

plenty of seedlings can be raised.

The plants are perennial but losses occur in winter, and something like 10–15% will expire during a British winter. The following season the plants commence flowering by the late spring and continue throughout the summer into autumn. The blooming is successional with flowers appearing soon after the previous stems have finished but nevertheless it is important to cut off the old ones, not let them run to seed.

In subsequent years more losses will occur and the plants seem to get taller, a factor which some experts blame on a deterioration of the original strain. It is best, therefore, to make annual sowings.

LARKSPUR

The garden larkspur is generally thought to have originated from two species. The rocket or hyacinth-flowered larkspur coming from *Consolida ambigua* (*D. ajacis*) and the stock flowered or imperial larkspur being derived from *Consolida regalis* (*D. consolida*) although no doubt there have been interchanges to produce today's hybrids.

The rocket or hyacinth-flowered larkspur is a non-branching plant growing about 105 cm (3 ft) tall, producing a single spike with double flowers in shades of white, pink, mauve, blue and purple. It comes into bloom in early summer, slightly ahead of the stock-flowered or imperial larkspur. There is, also, a dwarf strain which has

The beautiful colour and its late flowering habit are 'Molly Buchanan's' best assets.

neat and compact little spikes of tightly-knit flowers in a wide range of colours.

The stock-flowered or imperial larkspur forms a tall branching plant 90–150 cm (3–5 ft) high with long spikes of double flowers in a similar colour range. Although mixed strains are usually offered, they do come true from seed and can be obtained in separate colours.

Both types of larkspur are very hardy and can be an asset in any garden, in the mixed border where they will bloom for several weeks, or as a cut flower where they last well in water. They are probably the type of plant to grow in decent sized groups, particularly the small dwarf rocket strain which will look so much better if planted rather closely together. An autumn sowing produces larger plants, with the imperial strain growing over 1.5 m (5 ft), which can make a magnificent group. Equally, larkspur can be a useful filler for blank spaces if initially grown in pots or boxes.

Larkspur do not like being transplanted but they are not fussy about soil, although they prefer an open, well-drained position. They can be sown in late summer or early autumn in the place where they are to flower. However, the soil must not be too heavy or waterlogged. The plants raised at this time grow up to 1.5 m (5 ft) tall and come into flower during early to mid-summer, usually lasting for 8 to 10 weeks. The seed should be sown reasonably thickly because not every one comes up, and thinning should be delayed until spring unless the seedlings are really packed together. Initially, they can be spaced 5 cm (2 in) apart and finally 23–30 cm (9–12 in) apart. The dwarf rocket larkspur needs to be closer, perhaps 10–25 cm (4–6 in), depending on size. Try not to thin when the soil is dry, because moist and warm conditions make the job easy and less traumatic for the seedlings. As always slugs can be a nuisance and should be guarded against.

A spring sowing is more certain but does not produce such good plants nor do they flower as soon – mid- to late summer as a general rule. A foolproof method is to sow the seed very thinly in peat pots filled with seed compost and then without any disturbance plant out when the seedlings are a reasonable size. Ensure that the compost in the pot remains moist until it is certain the roots have moved into the surrounding soil. The advantage of this is that there is no problem with weeds, whereas seedlings sown direct in the soil have to compete with all manner of weeds which seem to germinate quicker than the larkspur, making life difficult for the gardener both in spotting the seedlings and in pulling them out without pulling larkspur seedlings too.

Larkspurs are excellent material for flower arrangers and raised in rows and spaced 8 cm (3 in) apart in rows 60 cm (2 ft) apart will produce tall single spikes in profusion.

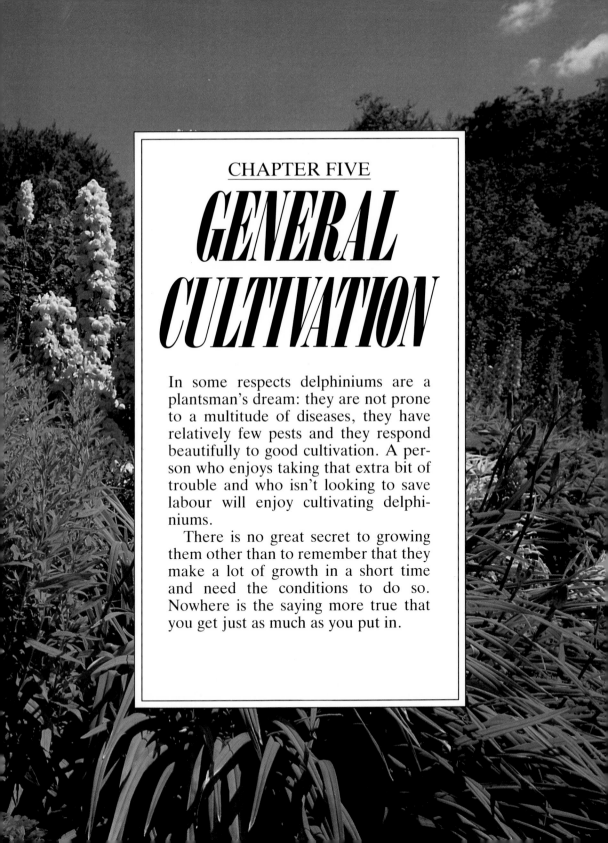

CHAPTER FIVE

GENERAL CULTIVATION

In some respects delphiniums are a plantsman's dream: they are not prone to a multitude of diseases, they have relatively few pests and they respond beautifully to good cultivation. A person who enjoys taking that extra bit of trouble and who isn't looking to save labour will enjoy cultivating delphiniums.

There is no great secret to growing them other than to remember that they make a lot of growth in a short time and need the conditions to do so. Nowhere is the saying more true that you get just as much as you put in.

SOIL

Delphiniums can be grown on all types of soil; over the years they have been cultivated successfully on chalk, heavy stiff clay, gravel, light loam, peat, sand and just plain dirt. Of course, to obtain worthwhile results these soils need cultivating as good delphiniums require a degree of good husbandry. Different soils require different degrees of treatment. The lucky gardener with really good loam can take it far easier than the poor devil with the sticky yellow clay but, provided the 'soil' is improved delphiniums can be grown.

SITUATION

The theory is simple: delphiniums require an open situation. They will not thrive if they are grown in heavy shade or under trees. Even if they get a certain amount of sun, delphiniums positioned beneath the branches of a tree will be drawn towards the light causing the florets to become 'gappy' with spaces between them revealing great areas of stem. Furthermore, they need plenty of water and that kind of position is invariably dry due to the leaves of the tree keeping the rain off and its roots taking what moisture there is. Having said all that, they do not need to be in full sunlight for the whole of the day. It is usually reckoned that they can flourish as long as they are not in shade for more than half the day. Indeed, it can be advantageous for them to be shaded from the hot mid-day sun because some cultivars, particularly pale pinks, can

bleach quite badly giving them a really washed-out look.

Delphiniums require plenty of water during their growing season and the wetter the soil can be kept the better. However, it is a different story in winter when waterlogged soil will unquestionably lead to losses. Soil which fails to drain fairly quickly and which still has puddles lying on the surface many hours after a downfall of rain is likely to need work on it. Adding plenty of humus will help and if conditions are really bad it might be as well to build up the level of the soil by adding more topsoil and compost or manure to create, in effect, a raised bed.

PLANTING TIME

At one time it was usual for nurserymen to send out new delphinium plants in autumn. This may be an ideal time for shrubs and trees but not for delphiniums. Because they remain dormant in the winter months it meant that from the time they were planted, until the spring, they sat in the cold wet soil without any new root growth at all. Not surprisingly losses were heavy due to them rotting away; only the plants sent out with large amounts of soil still around their roots survived easily.

Specialist delphinium nurserymen produce new plants from cuttings taken in early spring. The practice now is to send out these young plants in late spring and early summer and this is by far the best time to put them out into the open ground. The plants have almost a full growing season ahead of them and can, therefore, become well established before autumn and the winter dormancy. If they receive proper attention they could well produce a reasonable flower spike towards the end of the growing season. The great merit of this spring planting is that the plants will produce excellent spikes the following season.

This is provided they are well looked after initially. When the new plants are put into the soil they must be kept well watered until they are obviously growing away. When received the plants will be in pots. After planting out it is quite possible, particularly if they are in peat-based compost, for the pot-shaped block of compost around the roots to be absolutely dry although the surrounding soil is moist. While the roots remain within that original compost it is clear that the plant could suffer and possibly die if conditions become too dry. Before planting out takes place the plants should be given a thorough soaking, preferably by standing them in water. This ensures that the compost is thoroughly moist to start with, then watering should be done carefully to ensure that the original compost has not dried. Once the roots have ventured into the soil of the border watering is not so imperative but should not be neglected, particularly in hot dry weather or even during the overcast days of late summer when the skies are cloudy but little rain actually falls.

It does sometimes happen that planting cannot take place in late spring, early summer or even mid-summer either because the space is not available or because there simply isn't the opportunity. Obviously, the planting can still go ahead later and if the plants can get settled there may be no problem. A safer way which ensures survival during winter is to pot them on into larger pots, 25 cm (10 in) or 30 cm (12 in) for preference, using a soil-based compost. The pots can then stand in a sheltered position in the open until the following spring when the delphiniums will start to shoot. When the soil is suitable for planting they can then go out. This way you may lose a little time but the plants survive for sure.

GROUND PREPARATION

When preparing the ground for any plant, consideration has to be given to its requirements. Does it hate lime, does it need feeding etc? In the case of the delphinium we have seen that it needs plenty of water in summer but hates to be waterlogged in winter. It is also apparent that to produce a 1.5 m (5 ft) or 1.8 m (6 ft) flowered spike towards the end of early summer when the shoots only came through the ground in late winter, the plant will need plenty of nourishment. Furthermore, when a delphinium is planted it will remain in the ground for several years and will need sufficient nutrients to keep it going during its life span. With regard to alkalinity, it prefers a neutral to slightly acid soil but is not too fussy. The answer to most of the delphinium requirements is organic matter in the form of well-rotted compost or farmyard manure. Organic material added to the soil enables it to hold more water, useful to delphiniums growing in sandy soil. Such materials, even before they are broken down by earthworms and micro-organisms, act like a sponge, absorbing large quantities of water which the plants can use. Paradoxically, the soil drains better too.

Preparation of the soil is not a job to skimp. There is no going back on the situation once the plants are in place and no last minute applications of ferti-lizer will put matters right.

☐ TIMING OF THE PREPARATION

It is no good waiting until the moment of planting before deciding to prepare the ground. Freshly dug soil is loosely packed and will sink, sometimes as much as 8–10cm (3–4in). It does not take much imagination to think what will happen to the newly planted delph-iniums as the soil subsides around them. Accordingly, preparation should take place well in advance to allow the soil to settle and the worms to start work in order that it can become the perfect growing media. If starting on a poor soil dig in autumn. Well cultivated or sandy soils can be left until early spring.

☐ DIGGING

As already mentioned delphiniums re-quire a soil which is fertile, friable and well drained. Digging is done to help to achieve these aims; just how much depends on the existing condition of the border. Basically, soil can be seen as consisting of three layers or strata. The uppermost level, the topsoil, is from where delphiniums obtain most of their food so it should be dark with humus, fertile and as free from perennial weeds as it is possible to get; the bottom layer, the subsoil, is more inert, being clay, chalk or gravel but should allow good drainage; the middle layer is a combina-tion of the previous two, hopefully being on its way to becoming topsoil. Each of these layers needs to do its job and digging is done to improve or re-adjust any shortfalls. With an old established garden the soil will be easily workable and will drain quickly but it will have been cropped extensively. The main requirement, therefore, will be to add plenty of plant foods and organic material to the top layer. This will help to feed the delphiniums and help to retain water. A sandy soil will be simi-lar: it too will drain and will be friable. Again, organic matter needs to be added to the topsoil. New gardens with virgin soil could be fertile but the top layer will need breaking up to obtain a reasonable tilth for planting. One type of soil which certainly requires different treatment is that where a thin layer of topsoil covers chalk. No attempt should be made to break up the chalk but instead efforts should be devoted to build up the depth of the topsoil by adding further soil and organic matter.

In each of these cases there is usually no need to touch the subsoil. It is only when the drainage is bad that it becomes necessary to dig down two spades in depth to break up the hard pan of clay.

(Opposite) *'Olive Poppleton' has pretty florets and graceful spikes but its bottom petals can drop early.*

The actual digging should be done carefully, taking plenty of time. It then becomes less back breaking and gives the opportunity to remove every bit of perennial weed. Bindweed and ground elder can be extremely troublesome when found growing amongst delphiniums so that the attention given to eradicating them at the very start is time well spent.

□ **MANURE**

Soil consists of sand, silt and clay particles, organic matter plus a busy population of worms, insects, bacteria and fungi. A good soil has a lot of space too. Earthworms and insects move around in the soil leaving air-filled spaces which are so important in forming and maintaining a good soil structure. These spaces allow water to run away, provide passages for oxygen and carbon dioxide to enter or leave, and allows roots to penetrate the soil easily. Organic matter is important because it is used as a food by a variety of organisms; some insects and the earthworms break it down through their digestive systems, while other micro organisms continue the work. The result is a complex, dark brown, organic material known as humus which combines with the mineral part of the soil to stabilize the structure.

It follows, therefore, that the more organic matter that is added, the more earthworms, insects and micro organisms will inhabit the soil. This not only ensures that the soil remains space-filled but encourages bacteria and fungi which provide chemicals that stick the soil together.

A soil with adequate humus is very easy to dig. The spade will go in easily and, provided the soil is not too wet, will not cling to the blade. When turned over good soil should break down into small lumps and it will recover quickly after it has been compacted. The sure test follows rain for it should keep its structure and not form a hard, impermeable surface.

The most convenient source of organic material is the compost heap and well-rotted compost worked into a border being prepared for delphiniums is most beneficial. The problem with compost making is that there is never enough material to compost and, by the time decomposition has finished, there is precious little to go a long way. However, there are other materials which even these days can still be found. The best is farmyard manure but a good few delphinium enthusiasts swear by mushroom compost and, of course, there are proprietary concentrated manure-based composts although they tend to be expensive to use.

As far as delphiniums are concerned generous amounts of organic material incorporated in the topsoil will be repaid with interest when the plants produce large and beautiful spikes. When digging, a layer of manure or compost 8–10cm (3–5in) deep should be placed at the bottom of the trench and well forked in. Then the trench should be filled in and more organic material distributed thoroughly in the soil. Finally, incorporate a handful of bone-meal per square metre. This slow-acting fertilizer will benefit the soil for some time.

PLANTING

Prior to planting the soil should be lightly forked over and any weeds removed. The actual process of planting is mostly a matter of commonsense. A hole, sufficiently large to take the root ball without it being crammed, is made and the plant placed in the hole. A small handful of blood, fish and bone in and around the hole will encourage growth. Delphiniums received from a nursery are usually in pots and the planting depth is obvious: the level of soil and compost in the pot should be the same. If plants are being moved around the garden the same rule applies. Confusion might arise when plants are obtained with little or no soil on them but in general delphiniums should not be planted too deeply. The crown of the plant or, in the case of a seedling or rooted cutting, the base of the growing shoot should be at ground level. On the other hand if planted too shallow the roots will be exposed. After planting the soil should be firmed around the plants and then, most importantly, they should be well watered. If the plants are to settle in their positions they will need further waterings and to neglect this factor is to flirt with failure.

Given the choice the sooner delphiniums are planted in their final position the better. This site should be selected with great care for there is no doubt that the older a plant is, the longer it takes to get over a move. A young seedling or cutting establishes itself quickly and, given due attention, will flourish in the years to come.

□ PLANTING ESTABLISHED DELPHINIUMS

Delphiniums that have become well established resent being moved and take a long time to get over it and sometimes never flower as well as they did. The younger delphiniums are when they are transplanted the better. Nonetheless, there are occasions when mistakes have happened or when a change forces the issue, that old plants have to be planted elsewhere. It can be done and has been done successfully provided the plant is dug up with as large a ball of soil as possible and, most importantly, that the plant is kept well watered before, during and after the move.

□ PLANTING DISTANCES

Most modern gardens have too little space and so enthusiasts have to plant their delphiniums close together. In some respects this is no bad thing as a close group can look very good, but if the concern is quality rather than quantity, plants set further apart are better. A border devoted entirely to delphiniums would ideally need them to be 90 cm (3 ft) apart to grow at their best. However, this is space consuming and is not really required for delphiniums growing in a mixed border where 60 cm (2 ft) is far more realistic. It may be that even that amount of space is unavailable but delphiniums are adaptable and surprisingly good plants can be grown even closer together. In the end it probably comes down to the size of the garden and the room that can be given to delphiniums. However, it may be encouraging to note that several

'Pericles' has been underrated over the years but is a reliable, worthwhile plant.

amateur breeders grow their seedlings very close together, sometimes less than 30 cm (12 in) apart. This is obviously to ascertain the worth of the seedlings but the resulting display is often breath-taking.

□ FILLING SPACES

It sometimes happens that a plant dies, leaving a nasty gap in the border. There is not really much of a problem if the plant is new and provided it hasn't died from being in completely the wrong place, for example beneath a huge tree, then another can be put in its place. However, when the deceased was an old established plant it pays to be a little more careful. There is no doubt that delphiniums, along with most other plants, do not thrive in soil which has held other delphiniums for a number of years. The best answer is to put some-thing else in. A fairly unsatisfactory alternative is to dig out a hole as wide and as deep as possible and fill it with fresh and fertile topsoil which has not had delphiniums growing in it. Leave this to settle for a couple of weeks and then plant the new replacement.

SPRING CARE

In late winter, sometimes earlier or later depending on season and location, the first signs of growth appear and the new shoots break through the ground. This is the start of a hectic period when various jobs should be undertaken. The quality of the flowers to be seen in the coming summer depends very much on the attention given to the plants during these early stages of their development.

The first requirement is to give the plant encouragement. A feed of nit-rogen boosts growth of root, stem and foliage and this should be given when the new shoots reach approximately 5 cm (2 in) high, usually in mid-spring. Dried blood is an organic nitrogenous fertilizer which is easily applied and is quick acting. It is expensive, but a cheaper inorganic substitute is sulphate of ammonia: 60 g (2.10 oz) of either needs to be evenly sprinkled around plants and lightly forked in. If there is no rain within a few days the fertilizer should be watered in with a canful of water. There are a couple of points to note. Firstly, take care with the sulphate of ammonia not to get any on the foliage. Secondly, both fertilizers are 'strong' types for strong healthy plants and there is little they can do for weak or ailing plants. Dried blood can be given to young seedlings or cuttings but at only half the quantity. Finally, re-member that fertilizers like these are no substitute for good soil preparation.

THINNING SHOOTS

The next job is thinning and it is one that is essential if good spikes are to be achieved. Delphiniums produce a num-ber of shoots and an established plant could give over a dozen. If these are all left to grow, the result will be lots of thin, spindly spikes. There will be plenty of flower but with so many stems they will be crowded together. There is no doubt that thinning a few of these shoots will improve the look of the plant. The

(Opposite) *Recently introduced, 'Rosemary Brock' has attracted much attention and looks to have a good future.*

(Above) *The eye-catching 'Sandpiper' flowers early and is easy to grow well.*

question is just how many to remove (Fig. 3). It does depend on several factors: the vigour of the plant, the age of the plant, on whether it is being grown for the border or as a feature plant. Obviously, it becomes a matter of judgement and choice but the golden rule is not to over thin. A good tip is to leave one stem more than finally required. The final thinning can be done at the time of staking when a final selection can be made of those stems which look likely to be worthy of the border. Caterpillars and slugs have a nasty habit of damaging the most precious of spikes, the very one due to astound friends, and a spare can come in very handy.

Rather like pruning roses, each plant must be assessed individually. A new plant has not got the wherewithal to carry the number of spikes that an older established one can and so should be thinned more drastically. One planted the previous year should be restricted to no more than two spikes, whereas an older plant can have five or six. A strong-growing plant can also have more than one which is less vigorous. Exhibitors take more drastic steps and reduce the shoots to a few but there is a certain limit and it does not follow that a strong-growing plant which is thinned down to one stem would produce a super spike. It would in fact probably have a terrible ill-formed, ill-growing one with florets all over the place and fasciated into the bargain.

The job of thinning is simplicity itself and merely consists of taking a sharp knife and cutting the unwanted shoots right back to their base. It should be

3. **Thinning**
(a) Before thinning, with the plant strength going into six shoots.

(b) Three shoots have been trimmed so that the remaining three can grow stronger.

done early when the new shoots are only an inch or so high. There is a temptation, particularly if the weather is bad, to wait until the shoots are 15–23 cm (6–9 in) high but this is wasting the plants' energies and tends to leave the stems weak and thin at the base. It is feasible and possible to combine thinning and taking cuttings using the surplus shoots, but care is required (see Chapter Six).

A certain pattern can be followed when it comes to the selection of which shoots to remove. First the weakest shoots are taken out and then, if there are still too many left, the ones growing in the centre of the plant can be removed. In an ideal world this would leave exactly the right number of shoots evenly spaced around the crown. Unfortunately, in reality there may well be too many shoots remaining, in which case the best ones should be left despite the fact they may all be situated on the same side of the plant, for as the spikes grow taller they can be spaced and positioned by judicious staking.

STAKING

Let's face it, staking delphiniums is a nuisance and nobody enjoys doing it. However it is part of growing delphiniums and pleasures of most kinds have a price to pay. Making sure the spikes keep upright is essential because unless this is done properly, as the delphinium spikes get taller so a mere puff of wind will knock them over. Once they have gone down no amount of correction work will get them to look quite the same.

There is, however, no need to make hard work of the job. The first requirement is to do the staking at the right time, when the spikes are about 23–30 cm (9–12 in) tall. Three 1.2 m (4 ft) canes should be pushed into the ground around the plant to a depth of about 15 cm (6 in). At this time of the season the ground is usually still quite soft so it should not be too difficult. Thick garden twine should then be tied to the canes at about 23 cm (9 in) from the ground so as to encircle the stems of the plant (Figs. 4 & 5). The stems are pliable and, if necessary, can be tied to the string or canes in order to persuade them to grow in the right direction. This first enveloping tie should be sufficient until the bloom spike appears when a similar tie

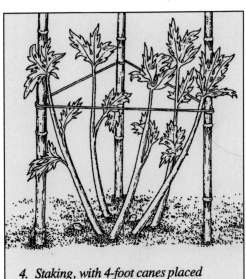

4. *Staking, with 4-foot canes placed around the plant and an encircling tie made to support the growing shoots.*

The colour of 'Spindrift' can vary according to circumstance, making it an interesting plant.

'Strawberry Fair' is a very reliable plant which rarely fails to make a good display.

5. **Staking**
(a) *Good staking, with the canes steadying the spikes but hidden by the foliage.*

(b) *Bad staking, with far too tall and heavy stakes used.*

can be made at a height just below the bottom florets. Once again this should encircle all the stems. With the majority of plants two ties are adequate but if they grow taller and it looks as though another tie would be useful take no chances and position a third tie around them. The whole aim is to provide a cage around the plant to keep the stems in position but at the same time allowing a certain amount of movement in windy weather. The thing to remember is that in the early stages of development a stem growing in the wrong direction can be fixed to grow correctly, but once the spike has started to extend it is too late and any attempt at correction will result in a bent spike.

There are, of course, other methods of staking. For exhibitors or those with only a few plants there is the one cane to a spike method. A 1.2m (4ft) cane is pushed into the ground close to the spike when it is 23–30cm (9–12in) tall and a tightish tie is made. This first tie is critical: it must not be too tight so as to restrict the growth of the stem but it should steady and position the spike. A second loose tie should then be made when the bloom spike starts to appear. The twine should be fixed to the cane but merely looped around the stem. The reason for this is that if the tie is too tight the spike will snap at the juncture as soon as a stiff breeze blows. Delphinium spikes are surprisingly springy and can sway considerably in a wind without sustaining damage and the purpose of the second tie is to act as a restraint and yet to provide room for movement within certain limits.

A further method of supporting delphiniums, often adopted by gardeners with large gardens and little time, is to use peasticks. By sticking these in the ground when the growth is short the stems can grow through the twigs and so allow the spikes to be held by the twigs. Unfortunately, this method cannot be said to do much for the look of the plant before flowering and very little more when it is.

There are patented plant supports available and they can do the job very well although no better than canes. They are rather expensive but do last for a long time. They may well be worth consideration by the gardener who is short of time but not of money.

SURFACE CULTIVATION

Delphiniums in a border should not require a great deal of attention except regular hoeing to keep the weeds at bay. But the soil can become compacted because with delphiniums requiring thinning, staking and plenty of water, there will be a good deal of tramping going on around the plants. But regular summer hoeing is essential even if the soil occasionally needs breaking down with a fork. This is because the delphinium's canopy of leaves is not sufficiently thick to prevent weeds growing beneath them and the conditions are ideal for weeds to germinate so that it does not take long for the soil around the plant to become weed infested. Equally,

once they have become established it is hard work to restore the border.

A mulch of good compost or farmyard manure can save a lot of this labour and a layer of 8–10cm (3–4in) thick around each plant applied during midspring when the soil is moist on the surface will conserve moisture, provide food and suppress weeds.

WATERING AND FEEDING

During the spring the delphiniums will be growing strongly and it pays handsome dividends if they are given a little attention. Some growers maintain that for average requirements in the garden, provided initial soil preparation was adequately done, further feeding and watering is unnecessary. It is certainly true that the delphiniums will not be disappointing but a true plantsman wants to see plants growing to their best advantage and will surely be prepared to assist them to do so.

No less than three weeks after the spring feed of dried blood and when the plants are approximately 45cm (18in) high, an application of a general fertilizer can be given. Growmore is perfectly acceptable and should be applied at 60g (2.10oz) per plant; if a proprietary fertilizer is used then the makers instructions should be followed. For the organic gardener the choice is a little bit more difficult. Fish blood and bone would do the job but it does sometimes contain inorganic chemicals.

A similar feed can be given two weeks later and if the season is dry they should be watered in although in the circum-

(Above) *The bright and showy
'Sungleam' needs good treatment to bring
out its best.*

(Opposite) *'Tiddles' has somewhat
unusual florets in that they have a 'double'
appearance.*

stances it might be better to use a liquid feed, following the maker's instructions. This should be generous with each plant receiving at least 9 litres (2 gal).

When the flower spikes are extending and before the colour starts to show, a feed of sulphate of potash can be given at the rate of 30–60g (1.10–2.10oz) per plant. The purpose of this is to harden the stems and to brighten the colours of the florets. Once again, unless there is plenty of rain the feed will require watering in.

DISBUDDING

As the flowers develop on the spike a number of side shoots or, as they are usually called, laterals, begin to appear. The numbers vary depending on the cultivar: sometimes there are a dozen or so and sometimes as few as three. These laterals extend the flowering season by providing a good display of colour after the main spike has finished. They are also much in demand by flower arrangers. If there are a lot of laterals on a spike, quite a good case can be made for removing a few. When too many are left, and occasionally a plant will produce an extraordinary number, they can hide the main flower spike and can get tangled with its florets. If a few laterals are removed those remaining will improve in quality; the fewer shoots that are left, the better those left will be. Taking them off is simply a matter of pinching out the embryo shoots with the finger nails although a small pair of scissors will do just as well. Those laterals directly below the bottom flow-

er buds are the ones to remove – in other words, work down so that the bottom ones are left. As a final note, delphiniums being grown for exhibition purposes should have all their laterals removed.

AFTER FLOWERING

Fame tends to be fickle and fleeting and after their magnificent display delphiniums frequently get neglected and left to fend for themselves. This is most unfortunate because a little care and attention can make a lot of difference to the following season's results.

Once the flowers have finished, cut off the spikes to a level below the laterals and let the stems die down naturally. They can eventually be cut right down when the leaves have withered and dried. Plants sometimes flower again in late summer or autumn and there is no harm in this – indeed it can be a decided benefit. If a plant looks as though it wants to flower, the old stem should be cut away to allow the new growth room to flourish. It is probably unwise to feed to encourage growth, because clearly the plant has enough energy to enable it to flower without further boosting. For the same reason it is not good policy to cut the stem down just to encourage a second flowering because the plant is clearly not ready to send up new growth. Some cultivars regularly bloom twice in a season but it is usually newly planted young seedlings and new cuttings which flower again.

The most important job during the late summer months is ensuring that the plants do not dry out. Conditions can be extremely dry at this time and although the plants do not need as much water as they did when throwing up flower spikes, they certainly need sufficient water to enable them to build up their strength for the next season's efforts.

WINTER CARE

Delphiniums are absolutely hardy and in their dormant state are quite immune to damage from severe frost. There is certainly no need to protect delphiniums from the cold. Young growth produced as a result of a false spring may be nipped by a sudden hard frost but the actual plant does not suffer. Indeed, most experienced growers believe that they sustain fewer losses during a hard cold winter than they do when the weather remains mild but wet.

The actual work needed to be done during the winter months is very little because the plants die down and go into dormancy at any time from early autumn onwards. There may be some secondary growth still green in early winter if the weather has been damp and warm but generally speaking the autumn tasks are one of clearing and cleaning up. The stems need to be cut right down, while dead leaves and rubbish should be cleared away. Admittedly, it does sound a little perfectionist and the benefits have never been proved, but because the stems are hollow and water can accumulate in them and cause rotting, some growers think it a good idea to plug the stems with something like putty or cover them with aluminium foil. This may well be worth doing provided there are not too many plants, especially when named cultivars are expensive.

It really does pay to weed the border thoroughly in autumn as it stops the ground becoming over grown and forking around the plants helps the winter rains to drain away.

There is one aspect of winter care which is of paramount importance to the delphinium grower and that is slug eradication. Everyone knows that slugs love to eat delphiniums but what is often not realized is that most damage is done in the late winter and early spring when there is nothing visible on the soil surface. This is the time when young shoots and eyes are developing ready to emerge later. It is the time too when the slugs, particularly the small black keeled one, are down below chewing away, unless the gardener prevents them. Ways and means of destroying slugs are discussed later but keeping the border tidy reduces the number of hiding places for slugs and snails. Covering the crowns with sharp sand or, better still, horticultural grit is also a deterrent but should not be entirely relied upon. This needs to be done thoroughly to be any use at all. First the top covering of soil needs to be removed to expose as much of the crown as possible. Then, give the plant a good soaking with a liquid slug destroyer to destroy all the slugs and their eggs lurking down below. Failure to do this will mean that the gritty covering will merely provide a roof for their nefarious activities. Finally, cover the crown with the grit. This may be

Cool 'Turkish Delight' has neat tapering spikes and makes a nice contrast to darker shades.

A 'patriotic' border of delphiniums, red phlox and white red roses.

washed away by the rain during the season so may need to be topped up once or twice. Unfortunately, this may not provide total protection and it is advisable to use other methods in the continuous war against slugs.

PESTS

On the whole delphiniums are not prone to a lot of pests and diseases. They have a major enemy, slugs, but any other problems that a delphinium grower may encounter are unlikely to be serious.

□ SLUGS AND SNAILS

Delphiniums and slugs go together, unfortunately. Slugs love to eat delphiniums and the conditions which suit delphiniums are just fine for slugs, too. Some areas are almost without slugs and snails – gardens on chalk are sometimes like this. New gardens can also be without them. The trouble is that once the humus content is increased and cultivation really begins so the slugs and snails move in.

It is probably the small keeled slug which does the most damage to delphiniums. In early spring they attack the dormant eyes of the plant and because this happens underground the grower can be completely unaware. The first inkling that anything is wrong comes when the shoots fail to appear on time. The grey field slug and the black field slug live mostly above ground but they too adore new shoots and many a grower has found boxes of seedlings devoured in the night by these creatures. Snails are possibly less of a problem but they too can consume seedlings and shoots. And all of them seem capable of climbing high into the mature plants to eat the embryo flowers.

The only answer is prevention, because to wait until damage occurs can be fatal. The methods available to control slugs and snails are numerous but they can be divided into three groups:

SLUG PELLETS

The majority of slug pellets consist of mainly metaldehyde, and they are usually small and coloured to make them unattractive to birds. The usual practice is to scatter them around and if they are not left in heaps but spread thinly they will not be eaten in quantity by pets and wildlife. The slugs and snails, on the other hand, are attracted to them and killed. The pellets soon disintegrate, especially after rain, so that to be an effective control fresh

---

NON-CHEMICAL METHODS IN THE SLUG WAR

The following have varying degrees of success but can be helpful.

Beer traps
Crushed eggshells
Grapefruit & orange skins
Lime surrounding plant
Plastic rings cut from bottles surrounding plants, (useful for seedlings)
Soot
Zinc strips ringing plant

applications should be made regularly – perhaps fornightly, or sooner if it has rained. Dead or seemingly dead slugs should be collected because they do sometimes recover if the conditions are damp. It also prevents them being eaten by hedgehogs which is possibly unlikely but not worth chancing.

There are other pellets on sale which contain methiocarb. These are more lethal to slugs and snails and to other creatures as well, including some in the soil. The same procedures should be followed with meticulous care.

LIQUIDS

There are several controls which can be watered on the plants. The big advantage is that they can reach the parts that other methods cannot. The disadvantage is that to be really effective the soil has to be saturated with the liquid. One of the proprietary killers contains metaldehyde and it is easy to use but rather expensive; in fact the method as a whole does become very expensive if a number of plants are to be treated.

Another liquid slug killer contains aluminium sulphate and copper sulphate. Once again it is easy to use and is most effective if used weekly during vulnerable periods such as early spring just before the new shoots are due. It is possible to purchase aluminium sulphate and, when diluted at a rate of 60 g (2.10 oz) per 4.55 litres (1 gal) it makes at most a good winter control. It should be used during early to mid-winter when the plants are completely dormant and it will kill most of the slugs it comes into contact with. What is more its astringent action will destroy any slug eggs. However, to reach the plant's crown where the slugs are harbouring the soil needs to be well soaked and because aluminium sulphate is acidic this can cause the soil to become acid if used to excess.

OTHER CONTROLS

The use of sharp sand or horticultural grit to cover the crowns in winter has already been mentioned but there are other methods which can be very useful. Using discarded grapefruit skins to trap slugs works quite well provided they are collected and destroyed. A plastic cup sunk into the ground and filled with beer traps slugs by the score but a recent test showed that many beneficial insects are killed as well. A surprisingly large number of slugs and snails can be collected by taking a walk among the delphiniums when the soil is warm and wet.

□ CATERPILLARS

Caterpillars are unlikely to cause extensive damage to delphiniums but they have an unerring 'nose' for the good plants and it is very aggravating to find that a choice cultivar has had its best spike half chewed away by one. The moth lays its eggs on the leaves and in the flower buds during late spring. They hatch within a week and the 1-2 cm (⅜ to ¾ in) long, dark brown or green caterpillars then proceed to eat the leaf or, worse still, the embryo flower buds. Once noticed they are fairly easy to control: the usual sign is a chewed leaf or one that is rolled up. A dusting with

The rose 'Iceberg' makes an effective companion for the blue delphiniums.

An oasis of colour in the city, Dora Larkan's garden at Canterbury.

derris dust or similar will often do the trick. Failing that a good spray with a suitable insecticide finishes them off.

DISEASES AND PLANT PROBLEMS

□ CUCUMBER MOSAIC VIRUS

All plants can suffer from viruses of various kinds and delphiniums are no exception but there is little cause for growers to worry about it. The cucumber mosaic virus is the one that might affect delphiniums and it can be recognized by the plants having weak growth with sickly looking foliage, mottled and narrow leaves and florets which are distorted with narrow and wavy petals. The incidence is very hit and miss – some gardeners never have it in their plants while others have it on a few plants. The reason why the disease spreads each year is not known; aphids have been blamed and this is possible, for although they do not favour delphiniums, they probably sample the sap before deciding to go elsewhere. This visit could be enough to do the damage. Whatever the cause, once virus strikes the only course of action is to dig out the stricken plant immediately and burn it straightaway. Hands should be washed before any other delphiniums are handled.

□ CROWN ROT

Crown rot is a disease of delphinium old age. It is usually evident in spring when the growth restarts and a plant or part of a plant suddenly wilts and eventually dies. On examination it will be found that the crown is a mass of black rotting tissues. It is degeneration of the crown and the cause is probably a collection of factors. The main one has to be the way the plant normally grows, which is producing new growth outward from the crown, leaving a dead centre. The older the plant the bigger this centre and rotting can begin here. Water entering the crown by way of the cut-down stems may contribute and certainly plants grown in waterlogged soil go down very quickly. Some growers blame overfeeding for excessive losses and there is no doubt that slugs can play a part too. Taking cuttings has also been blamed, the theory being that because bleeding occurs following the severing of the cutting the plant becomes dehydrated and the crown collapses.

The fact is that crown rot occurs and whatever the cause there is no remedy. The plant has to be dug out and destroyed. Its effects can be minimized by planting in well-drained soil and by periodically replacing old plants with new young ones.

□ MILDEW (*Erisiphe polygoni*)

Mildew is a grey/white powdery substance which usually afflicts delphiniums after flowering. It is mostly found on the leaves but occasionally it will strike early and then it can get on to the flowers as well. It is not harmful and if the attack happens after flowering, not worrying. Action needs to be taken if it starts to appear during flowering and a spray with a proprietary fungicide such as one containing benomyl will clear it.

Some cultivars are more prone to mildew than others and it is possible to reduce what after all is an unsightly problem by not growing these. They are mostly in the purple range – for example 'Chelsea Star' can suffer badly – but it is unfair to be specific because delphinium cultivars can get mildew in one garden and not in another. The only way to find out is by trial and error.

□ FASCIATION

Fasciation is the name given to a peculiar affliction which causes distortion of the stems and flowers of delphiniums. It is not a disease but merely abnormal cellular growth. The results can be many and varied with split and double stems, club-headed spikes and shepherd-crook spikes. Whiskery leaves instead of laterals is fairly common too. The cause is not known for certain but many experienced growers blame over feeding and sharp rises and falls in temperature during early spring for the occurrence in their plants. Once again some plants are more prone – 'Mighty Atom' seems to suffer badly during some seasons. There is nothing to be done when a spike begins to show fasciation, but rest assured that the plant could be perfectly normal again the following year.

□ BLACK SPOT (Bacterium delphini)

No relation to rose black spot, this minor disease reveals itself as dark blotches on the upper side of the delphinium leaves, and in some years the stems will be affected too. A spray with a systematic fungicide like benomyl will bring it under control but it does no permanent harm to the plant if left. Seasonal fluctuations seem to be the cause and so it can appear one year and not the next.

□ SOIL SICKNESS

It has been known for centuries that growing crops in the same place year after year reduces the yield. Rose growers are advised never to plant new roses in the spot where an old rose has just been removed. It is similar with delphiniums where a build up in the soil of minute eelworms (nematodes) gradually leads to a deterioration of flowering standard. This increase is gradual but it does mean that it is inadvisable to put new plants into soil which has recently had dephiniums growing in it. In effect it means that some sort of rotation should be adopted if delphiniums are to grow at their best. This is unlikely to cause any problem unless the garden is very small or delphiniums are being grown on a large scale.

□ DAMPING OFF

Damping off is a fungal disease which attacks seedlings, particularly if they are grown in unsterilized compost. Delphinium seedlings can be afflicted especially if they are sown early in the year under glass. The seedling leaves become white and wilt. Immediate action is required to save the rest of the seedlings and a watering with a liquid copper solution, following the maker's instructions, will usually do this.

CHAPTER SIX

PROPAGATION

One of the joys of gardening is producing your own plants whether from seed or from cuttings. It is so satisfying to watch a small seed turn into a large plant, or to see tiny roots emerge on a cutting. Once bitten by the bug it is easy to get carried away but friends are always pleased to have good delphiniums. Raising delphiniums from seed is reasonably easy, and taking cuttings can be slightly tricky; both offer just enough of a challenge to make any gardener feel proud at success. There are pleasures too. Seedlings are an uncertain quantity and waiting for the very first flowers is exciting. Whereas cuttings will be identical versions of known plants and satisfaction is gained from reproducing quality.

DIVISION

Dividing old delphinium plants is frowned upon by delphinium experts who say that taking cuttings is the only way to get more plants of a cultivar. But there are times when there simply isn't enough time in the day to bother with taking cuttings, and there are people, too, who cannot be bothered with all the fuss. If this is the case, then division is an answer.

Some herbaceous plants like Michaelmas daisies, helenium and hemerocallis are naturals for division because they have multiple crowns which can be pulled apart to form separate plants. A delphinium is somewhat different in that it has a central crown.

A young delphinium starts with one stem; the following year new growth is produced around the original stem and after several years the plant has formed a large clump with a centre which is, to all intents and purposes, dead. To divide the clump by chopping up the crown is useless because it will be a case of replanting a bit of worn out plant which will probably rot anyway. To do the job properly it must be done in early spring. The plant should be lifted and the soil washed away using the hose. With a sharp knife any healthy new shoots can be severed from the clump and trimmed so that any rot or decay is removed. The division should be planted as soon as possible.

SEED SOWING

Growing delphiniums from seed is a fascinating and extremely enjoyable pastime, not least because of the uncertainty over what will be obtained; a modern hybrid is a complex hybrid and the offspring are never identical, so the raiser can never be sure what he or she will get. Happily, raising delphiniums from seed is not difficult and does not require anything but the usual facilities. There is another bonus too in that it is a very cheap way of having plenty of nice plants for the garden.

THE SEED

The obvious way of obtaining delphinium seed is to buy it but this is not so straightforward as it might seem. Firstly, there is the question of viability because delphinium seed soon loses its ability to germinate. To remain fresh it needs to be kept in an airtight container in a refrigerator and it does not take a genius to realize that packets of delphinium seed, perhaps not the fastest selling seed on the garden centre's shelf, could have been lying around for some time before purchase. This will not have helped its germinating ability. (Incidentally, any seed not sown or seed which has been saved should also be kept in cool conditions. The packet needs to be put into a sealed jar or container and placed in the refrigerator but not in the freezer compartment.)

Secondly, there is the question of pedigree. Good seed needs to have good parents and elatum delphiniums have improved tremendously over the last few years. Some delphinium strains are awful, with misshapen spikes and florets of all sizes and shapes and they are not really worth growing. This means that to buy the best seed it must be purchased from a specialist source because that will have been harvested from the latest cultivars. Of course, this maxim does not apply to seed from delphinium species.

SOWING ANNUAL DELPHINIUM SEED

Several species are best treated as annuals; for details of saving these and larkspur, please see Chapter 4.

THE TIME TO SOW

Given the correct conditions delphinium seed can be sown at any time during the year but realistically only three periods make sense when it comes to growing the seedlings on.

Sowing under glass using a little gentle heat in mid-winter/late winter is probably the most difficult time because heat is required and because there are the problems later of ensuring the little seedlings do not receive setbacks, but it does give the plants chance to have nine months growing before dormancy and thus make fine plants for flowering the following year. There is also the bonus of having quite nice flower spikes in the late summer.

An easier time to sow is early to mid-spring when the routine of pricking out and planting into the open is more natural and the plants need less mollycoddling. The seed can be sown in pots which can be left in a garden frame to germinate or even in the open. Although, there is a good chance of seeing a few florets in flower the first year, the first chance of seeing a representative spike will not be until the following early summer.

For good germination there is no better time than late summer provided the seed has been harvested the same year. It is nearly impossible to buy fresh seed at this time, so it has to be collected seed. The young seedlings cannot be planted out in the same year but will have to remain in pots during their dormant period. Nonetheless, when they are planted out the following early spring they make fine plants and will give good spikes in late summer.

SOWING THE SEED

There is no particular secret to raising delphinium seed but as with many seeds some attention to detail pays dividends. They will germinate in any good compost suitable for sowing, whether it is soil based or peat based. It does really need to be a sterilized compost because germination takes three weeks and weed seeds will take less, besides which unsterilized soil may contain soil borne diseases, even insects and slug eggs. Whether to use soil-based or loam-based compost is a matter of choice and preference, as each has its own merits and the delphiniums seem to thrive in either. Some growers believe they grow quicker in peat-based composts but others think that the seedlings grown in it take longer to push their roots into the surrounding soil following planting out.

SEED SOWING TIMES, ADVANTAGES AND DISADVANTAGES

Sowing times	*Advantages*	*Disadvantages*
Mid-winter/ late winter	Nine months growth before dormancy. Flowers to be seen in early autumn, i.e. nine months from sowing.	Heat required to germinate seed. Warmth needed to prevent any seedling setback. Germination possibly slow. Germination possibly poor. Damping off more likely.
Mid-spring	Can be sown in pots standing in open. More natural cycle of growing with pricking out and planting out. Soil ideal for planting out in late spring.	No representative spikes until following mid-summer
Late summer	Excellent germination from collected seeds. Temperature right for germination and seedling growth. Representative spikes the following mid-summer	Seedlings need cover over winter and will be hanging around for five months before planting. Fresh seed required but not available commercially.

It is usual to sow the seed in pots or seed pans; seed boxes may also be used although they are often a little too shallow, delphiniums needing a minimum depth of 8 cm (3 in). Whatever the container, they should be thoroughly washed because problems can be transmitted and it is as well to take no chances. If soil-based compost is used a layer of well-draining material should be put in first. (The instruction used to be 'crock the pot well' but with so much plastic about, old bits of clay pot are difficult to find, but something like peat or perlite does well enough.) Peat-based compost does not need this but because delphiniums require moist compost a layer of perlite at the bottom can help. The delphiniums seem to like some perlite added to the compost itself, because their roots invariably make for it. Fill the container with compost, lightly firm and level the surface so that it is about 1.25 cm (½ in) from the top.

The seed can then be sown and as it is fairly large it can easily be placed evenly. Life is so much easier at the pricking out stage if the seedlings are scattered thinly rather than all growing together (Fig. 6). Sprinkle a *thin* covering of compost over the seeds: it should be no more than the thickness of the seed itself.

The container should then be watered, preferably by standing it in 2.5 cm (1 in) of water for approximately one hour, but a careful and thorough watering with a fine rose will do if time is short. The compost must be thoroughly moistened because the seed will not germinate in dry compost; on the other hand it must not be saturated. A piece of cling film should then be stretched over the pot.

What happens next depends on the time of sowing. For a mid-winter sowing the container can go into the propagator, although some people have been known to use airing cupboards. The required temperature does not have to be too high: 15°C (60°F) is ideal but if it drops below 10°C (50°F) for any length of time germination will be delayed. With a mid-spring sowing the pot can go into a frame, if available, or something like an apple box covered with a sheet of glass. It is quite possible to get good results by placing the pot inside a polythene bag and sealing it up, and then putting it in a spot in the garden that does not get too much sun. The late-summer sowing needs to be kept cool and therefore a shady place should be found for the container in a frame or outside. It is not a bad idea to put it in a polythene bag to help retain moisture.

6. **Seed sowing**

(a) Seed should be sown thinly as well spaced seedlings are easier to prick out.

(b) The seed needs to be only lightly covered with compost.

PRICKING OUT

Germination usually takes place in three weeks but it can be sooner so it is as well to start checking after 14 days. The compost must not dry out so you should keep an eye on that too, but if the initial watering was done properly there should be no difficulties. The first signs

(Above) *A good display but these delphiniums, close to a wall, have been 'drawn up'*

(Opposite) *'The Heath', famous for its display of delphiniums, illustrates just what they offer the gardener.*

will be minor upheavals and then one or two seedlings will break the surface. Delphiniums tend to come through over a week or two rather than all together. This is a bit of a nuisance but as soon as even one comes through, the cling film must be immediately removed. A very important factor is to keep the young seedlings out of the direct rays of the sun as they will burn up very quickly. They must also have sufficient light or they will be drawn up, especially if conditions are too warm. The first seedling leaves, the cotyledons, have absolutely no resemblance to delphinium leaves, being plain and non-serrated (Fig. 7) but when the second leaves, which do look delphinium-ish, arrive pricking out needs to commence. If the seedlings are well spaced anyway this can be delayed until later, but the less

disturbance the plants have the better, and clearly older plants have more roots to be disturbed and to get entangled with those of their fellow seedlings. It is usual to prick them out into 8cm (3in) pots and again soil-based or peat-based compost can be used. It should be a compost suitable for pricking out young plants, one with sufficient fertilizer in it for them to thrive. Seed boxes can also be used for pricking out but they must be of sufficient depth, at least 6.5cm (2½in) deep. More seedlings can be grown in them but for the average gardener pots are preferable because it makes planting out so much easier with not having to fiddle about lifting and sorting out plants from a box. Whatever the container they should be filled in a similar way to those used for sowing. The method for actually pricking out is

7. **Pricking out**
    (a) *The initial seedling leaves called cotyledons are plain and non-serrated.*

    (b) *Small seedlings should be gently levered from the compost by means of a small dibber.*

straightforward. The seedlings are loosened with a small implement – a table fork is just the job – and then grasping them by the leaves, they can be lifted out and placed in the compost. They should then be gently firmed in and watered. Once again for watering purposes, placing the pots in an inch or two of water (Fig. 8) is best because it does not disturb the plants but a soaking using a watering can with a fine rose is perfectly adequate provided care is taken.

Once they are pricked out the seedlings can be kept in a place well out of the direct rays of the sun, and again a shady frame is perfect. But even at this stage the young plants are quite tough and as long as they have been hardened they do not need over protecting. They do need two things, however: to be kept well watered and to be kept free from the attentions of the local slugs and snails. An extra bit of attention in the way of a feed or two with a weak but suitable liquid fertilizer will help to promote good growth.

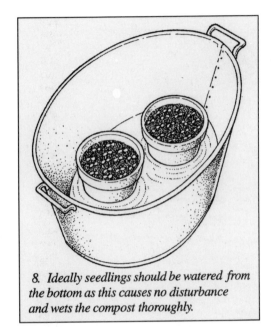

8. *Ideally seedlings should be watered from the bottom as this causes no disturbance and wets the compost thoroughly.*

PLANTING OUT

When to plant out is a matter of judgement. The seedlings have to be big enough to fend for themselves, the soil needs to be suitably warm and moist and the weather needs to be equable for plant and planter. Those seedlings resulting from the mid-winter and late summer sowings will probably be ready to go out just as soon as the weather and soil have warmed up a bit. On the other hand, the soil should be just right for the early spring sown seedlings just as soon as they are ready. It does not pay to plant out the young plants when they are very small because the slugs will eat them overnight but if they are left in their pots too long they will not get going when they are eventually placed. There is a balance to be struck between getting the plants into the open ground while they are young and easy to transplant, and being too small to survive.

TAKING CUTTINGS

Raising delphiniums from seed is fun but there is only one way to propagate a named delphinium so that new plants are identical and that is by taking cuttings. Dividing a delphinium is alright, but the quality of spikes

A brick wall provides a background for delphiniums, erigeron, Lychnis chalcedonica *and* Lychnis coronaria.

'Cupid' is a small but perfectly formed version of its bigger sisters growing behind.

obtained from the divisions is rarely as good as from the original plant. Obtaining delphiniums from cuttings is not as easy as they take a longer time to root than dahlias, chrysanthemums and pelargoniums and the cuttings are much harder to take. Nonetheless, if one or two basic rules are followed most gardeners can take them and a great deal of satisfaction is experienced when a number of delphiniums raised from cuttings are planted out.

The time to take cuttings is late winter/early spring although they can be taken quite readily later on. It has to be a time when the new shoots are just coming through the ground. The problem is that it is not possible to just cut off any shoot and root it. Delphinium stems are hollow and a cutting taken that way, although it might possibly root, would assuredly decay in the course of time. There is only one way to be certain of success and that is by ensuring the cutting has a solid base. To get this the shoot must be cut from the crown of the plant. This entails scraping the soil away from the crown until the place where the shoot actually starts growing from is revealed. Care needs to be taken not to break off any other fragile young shoots by accident. Then with a sharp knife the shoot can be severed at the point where it joins the crown. If a lot of cuttings are being taken the knife should be sterilized each time by wiping the blade with a tissue soaked in strong disinfectant. Good hygiene practice like this prevents passing disease from one plant to another. The severed end of the cutting should

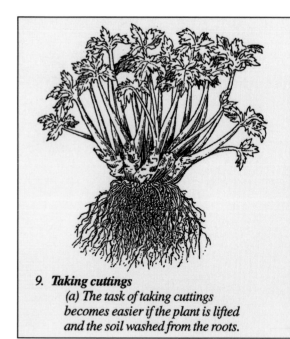

9. *Taking cuttings*
(a) The task of taking cuttings becomes easier if the plant is lifted and the soil washed from the roots.

always be inspected; if it has a solid white appearance it is perfect; if the hollow pithy centre shows, the cut has been made too high up the shoot and is useless; and if the middle shows black or brown there is crown rot in the cutting and it might as well be thrown away. It sounds depressing but after a little practice it becomes easier. The task becomes even easier if the plant is lifted and the soil washed from the roots (Fig. 9). All the bending about and scrabbling in the wet, cold soil is done away with and if the job can be done on the bench of a nice warm glasshouse the chance of getting acceptable cuttings increases. The snag with this is that the lifted plant will never be the same and will certainly not produce any decent spikes for

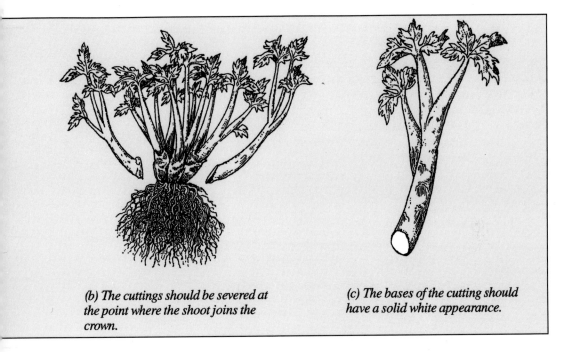

(b) The cuttings should be severed at the point where the shoot joins the crown.

(c) The bases of the cutting should have a solid white appearance.

another season, if at all. Growers who lift their plants in this manner take all the cuttings they possibly can and then dispose of the old crown. In theory any cuttings should be about 5 cm (2 in) to 15 cm (6 in) long but in practice longer ones will root fairly readily. With regard to thickness, shoots about 1 cm (½ in) thick appear to root quite quickly whereas very fat ones never will.

ROOTING CUTTINGS

Until 1970 most cuttings were rooted in a cold frame. The cuttings were inserted into sand or similar and were then watered and left to root. Some growers used to root them in the open ground with perhaps a jam jar to protect them.

The famous amateur enthusiast Ronald Parrett advocated rooting delphiniums in vermiculite. Quite a good method and one well worth doing is to fill 8 cm (3 in) pots with a mixture of half ordinary soil-based compost and half sand. The cuttings can be inserted singly in the pots and by using a shaded cold frame made to root in a few weeks. Care should be taken to see they do not dry out.

However, in the 1970 Delphinium Society Year Book a lady suggested rooting delphinium cuttings in cold water. This seemed an alien method because rotting is a problem with the hollow-stemmed shoots, but it was tried and found to work. Now most amateurs and some professionals use this method

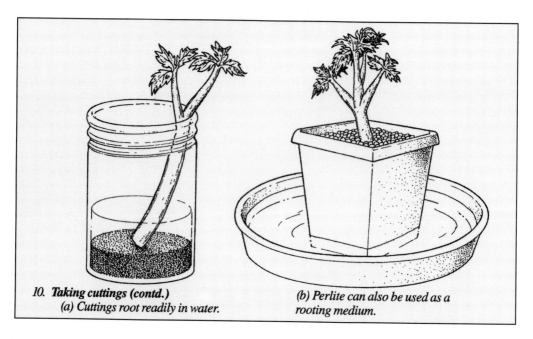

10. *Taking cuttings (contd.)*
(a) Cuttings root readily in water.

(b) Perlite can also be used as a rooting medium.

because it is easy and successful.

The technique is to stand the cuttings in water about 2.5 cm (1 in) deep with a layer of coarse sand at the bottom (Fig. 10*a*). Any container will do although a glass jar of some kind is probably best because the level of the water can be checked and, of course, whether any roots are forming. Any number of cuttings can be stood in a jar provided they are not too crowded. It is also preferable to keep one cultivar to a jar so as not to get muddled over which one is which. Once the cuttings are in the jars there is nothing to be done except to keep a check on the water level in the jars. The jars can be placed on a kitchen window sill or in the greenhouse, somewhere where they can get the sun. Roots will begin to form in three to five weeks depending on the time of year and the size of the cutting.

There is a variation to the cold-water method which is also very successful. With this method the cuttings are inserted into perlite held in pots or containers which have holes in the bottom (Fig. 10*b*). These containers are then placed into other containers holding about 1-2 cm (½–¾ in) of water. The size of the pots is not important although 8 cm (3 in) and 13 cm (5 in) are mostly used. The idea is that the water in the bottom tray will seep up through the perlite making each granule moist. The cuttings then have the best of both worlds: contact with the damp perlite and access to oxygen. Rooting takes as long as those in water but excellent roots form in the perlite. When the cuttings are carefully removed they have perlite clinging to them.

POTTING ON CUTTINGS

When the cuttings have made a few centimetres of root they should be potted on individually into 8cm (3in) pots filled with a suitable compost, taking care to crock or to place a layer of peat at the bottom of the pot (Fig. 11). Once again the choice is immaterial as to whether the compost is soil based or peat based. Care should be taken not to damage the new roots and the cutting should be firmly held in the compost. If the cutting is long it is as well to support it with a split cane. The pot or pots need to be well watered and once again the best method is to stand them in 2.5cm (1in) of water for an hour.

The pots should be kept in a shady place: a shaded cold frame or a position in the greenhouse where they avoid the

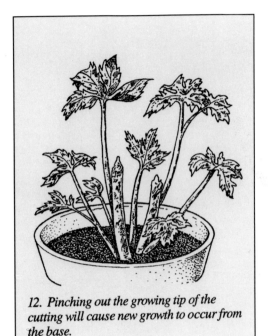

12. Pinching out the growing tip of the cutting will cause new growth to occur from the base.

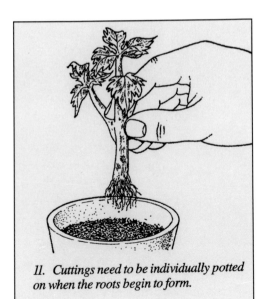

11. Cuttings need to be individually potted on when the roots begin to form.

direct sun. They must, of course, never dry out. Once the cuttings appear happy and are clearly growing, they can be gradually hardened off and the tip of each stem pinched out (Fig. 12). This will cause growth to form from the bottom and once new little green shoots appear around the base of the stem it is clear that the plant is established and ready to go out into the prepared border.

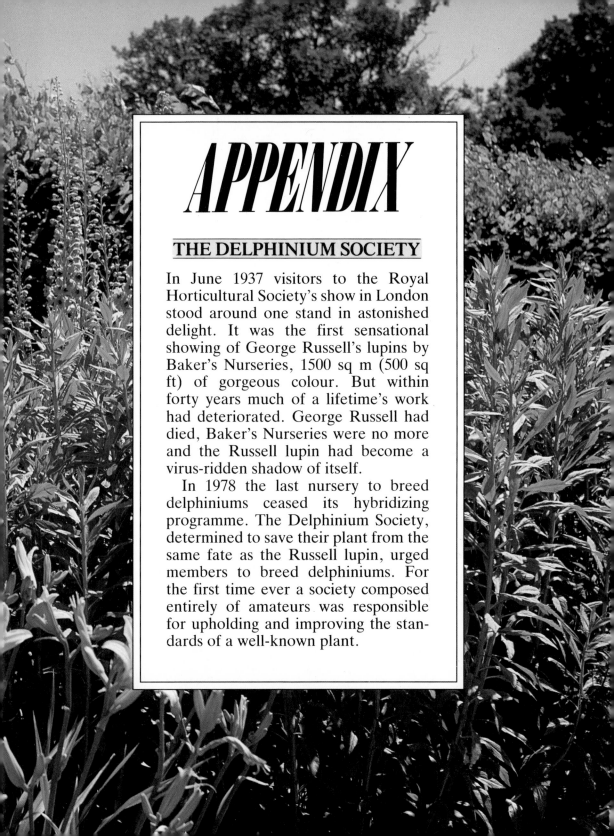

APPENDIX

THE DELPHINIUM SOCIETY

In June 1937 visitors to the Royal Horticultural Society's show in London stood around one stand in astonished delight. It was the first sensational showing of George Russell's lupins by Baker's Nurseries, 1500 sq m (500 sq ft) of gorgeous colour. But within forty years much of a lifetime's work had deteriorated. George Russell had died, Baker's Nurseries were no more and the Russell lupin had become a virus-ridden shadow of itself.

In 1978 the last nursery to breed delphiniums ceased its hybridizing programme. The Delphinium Society, determined to save their plant from the same fate as the Russell lupin, urged members to breed delphiniums. For the first time ever a society composed entirely of amateurs was responsible for upholding and improving the standards of a well-known plant.

THE DELPHINIUM SOCIETY IN THE PAST

In 1928 a group of men met for lunch in the Grosvenor Hotel, London. They were there to chat over an idea, the establishment of a British Delphinium Society. One was Charles Langdon, the resolute founder of Blackmore and Langdon, the greatest name in delphinium history. Another was Tommy Carlile, a nurseryman who specialized in herbaceous plants, while the other two were amateurs, Alec Moir and S. Halford Roberts. They chatted things over, finally deciding that a meeting should be called to see if there was sufficient interest in a society devoted to delphiniums. They were convinced that the nursery trade would be interested but wondered if there would be sufficient amateur support to make it a worthwhile proposition.

The meeting was duly held in September 1928 and those attending voted unanimously to form the British Delphinium Society. Alec Moir was to be the secretary and Charles Langdon the chairman. The aims of the new society were to encourage the production of new and improved varieties of delphinium, to collect and disseminate information about delphiniums, to undertake trials, to keep a register of recognized named varieties, to organize and hold exhibitions, and to publish an annual journal.

These objectives were, and are still being, achieved. The first show was held in 1929 and it was a fabulous affair with the R.H.S. New Hall filled with delphiniums. In 1930 the Year Book was published, the editor being S. Halford Roberts who retained the post for many years. Delphinium trials were held at R.H.S. Garden, Wisley.

During those pre-war days there was a great deal of interest in delphiniums, for those were the days of quite large estates and gardens. The shows reflected this by having classes which called for huge numbers of spikes, and by the number of specialist nurseries involved. For example, 13 nurseries staged exhibits at the first show.

Although the amateur membership gradually increased, the traders were very involved in the Society and in the Year Book there were even articles on book-keeping for the small nurseryman. Then the war came and things changed, with gardens being turned over to vegetables and labour becoming scarce. The British Delphinium Society survived, even managing to continue to produce its Year Book.

Following the war the membership increased but things had changed for ever; the days of the great private gardens were over and so many nurseries had disappeared. The 1951 show was cancelled due to a late season and no trade entries. And in 1952 only one nursery, Blackmore and Langdon, had a stand.

Crisis loomed and some members suggested winding up the Society and converting it into a hardy plant society. Meetings were held at the 1953 Annual General Meeting and the proposition was thrown out and another committee took over. This was a new era with two men leading the way: one was Reg Lucas and the other, Ronald Parrett, a first class writer with a flair for publicity. Ronald Parrett worked for Beaverbrook Newspapers and utilizing some *Daily Express* resources he edited a superb Year Book for 1954, full of colour and 160 pages long. The committee worked hard and membership expanded. In 1956 the name was changed to The Delphinium Society following the demise of an American Delphinium Society. Ronald Parrett continued as Editor until 1959. He became known as 'Mr Delphinium', appearing on TV, opening his wonderful garden and writing a superb delphinium book.

Once again there was a change because the Society finances had become stretched. Reg Lucas, a determined and dynamic man with an impish sense of humour, took charge and gradually the Society settled into a pattern of stability. It was now an amateur society in every sense, completely run by amateurs, for amateurs. There was only one delphinium nursery in existence, Blackmore and Langdon, and more and more enthusiasts discovered the joys of breeding and raising their own delphiniums. Then in 1978 Blackmore and Langdon decided to discontinue hybridizing.

The Delphinium Society now realized that it had an important role to play if delphiniums were not to deteriorate in the way the famous Russell lupin had. Was not the main aim of the Society 'to encourage the production of new and improved varieties of delphinium'? The response came as many fine delphiniums were raised and interest maintained.

THE DELPHINIUM SOCIETY NOW

Today the situation is very healthy. The membership is steady and the flower itself improving and becoming ever more popular. There are now several nurseries specializing in delphiniums.

The Delphinium Society prides itself on being friendly and forward thinking. It has members world wide, many in Canada and the United States of America and others in places as wide apart as New Zealand and Alaska. These overseas members receive Delphinium Society seed and the Year Book. Since the great years of Ronald Parrett, the Year Books have been the premier source of communication with members. The aim is to make them informative but readable, colourful and attractive.

The Society holds outings to gardens and nurseries and organizes symposiums. It also has a stand at the Chelsea Flower Show each year in order to meet members, enrol new ones, sell books and seed and generally to introduce delphiniums to the public. The Annual General Meeting now includes talks on delphiniums in its agenda, making for an interesting day.

An absolute highlight of the year is the Wisley weekend. The Society usually hold two shows, one being a competition held in the Royal Horticultural Society's hall at Vincent Square, Westminster, London, during one of the fortnightly shows. The other is the main

show held in the R.H.S. Garden, Wisley. Obviously members show their delphiniums, but there is also the opportunity to see the delphinium trials and usually the 'red' delphiniums which are growing at Wisley. Apart from this, it gives members the opportunity to chat and to talk to delphinium experts.

THE DELPHINIUM TRIALS AT WISLEY

Trials of delphiniums in the R.H.S. Garden at Wisley have been held since 1925. The trials are of importance to raisers because they provide a yardstick for comparison of new and old cultivars, plus a certain recognition should an award be received. They are equally important for enthusiasts who can see the plants growing while the award system gives a good guide to the merit of the cultivars.

Around 80 different cultivars are selected for trial each year, with older ones being rejected and new ones brought in. Nevertheless, some old friends like 'Alice Artindale' introduced in 1936 and 'Silver Moon' (1953) are, at the moment, still in the trials. Three plants of each cultivar are grown, all receiving the same treatment. A joint committee consisting of people from the Delphinium Society and the R.H.S. inspect the trials when the delphiniums are in flower and make awards to the outstanding ones. They are judged as garden plants and so it is not necessarily the biggest spikes which receive awards. It is usual to award a Highly Commended at first, then an Award of Merit can follow, while the premier award is a First Class Certificate given to only the outstanding cultivars.

(Opposite) Another view of 'The Heath' showing delphiniums and the variety of foliage shapes and textures.

INDEX

AUTHOR'S ACKNOWLEDGEMENT

The author would like to thank the following people who gave permission for their gardens and delphiniums to be photographed: Dora Larkan, Raymond Lister, Colin Parton, Mr and Mrs C. Pretzlik, and Richard Wainwright.

PUBLISHER'S ACKNOWLEDGEMENTS

The publishers gratefully acknowledge Nigel Moody for granting permission to reproduce the colour photographs on pp. 43, 44, 45, 48, 49, 52, 53, 56, 57, 60, 61, 68, 72, 79, 82, 84, 85, 88, 89, 92, 93 and 96. The photographs on pp. 8/9, 13, 16, 20, 22/23, 26, 33, 40/41, 64/65, 74/75, 97, 100, 101, 104/105, 110, 111, 114, 115, 120/121 and 124 were taken by Bob Challinor. All line drawings were drawn by Nils Solberg.